The Complete
High Holiday
Synagogue Companion

THE
JEWISH
LEARNING GROUP

THE COMPLETE HIGH HOLIDAY
SYNAGOGUE COMPANION
RABBI ZALMAN GOLDSTEIN

Revised and Updated Edition

Copyright © 2001-2014

THE
JEWISH
LEARNING GROUP
Tel. 1-(888)-56-LEARN
www.JewishLearningGroup.com
Email: Info@JewishLearningGroup.com

ISBN-10: 1-891293-10-9
ISBN-13: 978-1-891293-10-8

Acknowledgments

A special thanks to Rabbi-Dr. Nissan Mindel, past Editor-in-Chief of the Kehot Publication Society, for allowing me to include portions from his book, *My Prayer*, and *The Complete Story of Tishrei.*

To Yehudis Cohen, editor of the *L'chaim* publication, published by the Lubavitch Youth Organization, and Rabbi Eli Cohen, for providing many stories and ideas. To Rabbi Berel Bell for his inspiring essays.

To Rabbi Sholom Ber Chaikin, for giving so selflessly of his valuable time to read, amend, and refine the material presented here.

To the countless people and lay-leaders who have read and re-read the manuscript, and offered their creative ideas, advice, and whole-hearted encouragement.

A special thanks to two great proofreaders, my nephew S.Z. Goldstein and Shmuel Rabin. And to everyone else who helped make this book possible, thank you!

Using This Book

This book can be used as a pre-holiday study guide or alongside the prayer book during the services. Page numbers refer to the Hebrew/English edition of the High Holiday prayer book entitled, *Machzor for Rosh Hashanah Annotated Edition* (ISBN 0-8266-0160-X) and *Machzor for Yom Kippur* Annotated Edition (ISBN 0-8266-0161-8) published by the Kehot Publication Society, Brooklyn, NY. The (T:) symbol indicates transliterated prayers and their page number.

We have devised the following transliteration system to help readers accurately pronounce the Hebrew words of blessings and prayers presented in this book.

Hebrew:	Transliteration:	Example:
כ or ח	ch	Challah
ָ	ö	Of
ַ	a	Hurrah
ֵ	ay	Today
ֶ	e	Leg
ְ	'	Avid
ֹ or וֹ	o	Tone
ִ	i	Key
ֻ or וּ	u	Lunar
ַי	ai	Aisle
ָי	öy	Toy

Table of Contents

The High Holidays

The Jewish year begins with the *Yomim Norayim*, Days of Awe. They extend from Rosh Hashanah, the Day of Judgment, until Yom Kippur, the Day of Atonement. These ten days are a time of concentrated spiritual effort, permeated with the knowledge that everything we do during this time has the power to affect the coming year. The inspiration of these days awakens us to ever new possibilities for conducting our lives on a higher level, and we enter the new year prepared to improve our relationship both with God and with our fellow man.

The concept of *Teshuvah* (repentance or return), that is emphasized during these days is a positive one, permitting us to begin the year with a clean slate and the feeling of new beginnings. Prayer, *Tefillah*, is especially important during this time. Our prayers are both individual and communal, underscoring the fact that the fate of each Jew is fundamentally bound up with the fate of all other Jews and that we are all parts of one whole. This concept is also expressed in the giving of extra *Tzedakah*, charity, during these days (except on the Holiday itself).

The holiness of the Days of Awe is a prelude to the joy which follows during the holidays of *Sukkot* and *Simchat Torah*, Festivals of rejoicing. On Rosh Hashanah, as we affirm God's Kingship, we are filled with gladness and confidence that our prayers for a sweet year will be answered. Yom Kippur, the culmination of the days of

7

Teshuvah and the holiest day of the year, brings the certainty that we have been sealed for a good year.

Honey cake and sweet round *Challah* (special bread), giving charity and going to *Shul* (synagogue), holiday clothing and festive meals – are all part of the special time we call the Jewish New Year and the *Yomim Norayim.*

The experience of these days remains with us well into the year, providing inspiration and strength until a new cycle begins once again with another new year, each year bringing a new light and radiance as the cycle continues.

A Quick Prayer Primer

Odd Man Out

It may be your first time in a synagogue, or your hundredth, but the feeling can be the same. You say to yourself, 'I like it here, it feels good and I know I am doing the right thing, but I don't feel as if I am *really* participating, I don't feel that I really *connect*.'

You may find comfort in the following fact: An average 35-year-old observant Jew has prayed over 36,000 (!) services (three times a day on average). No wonder it appears to be so easy for him or her. Imagine how the Speaker of the House feels on his first day on his job in the Congress, and how comfortable he becomes at the end of his term. He memorized the protocol, he feels "at home."

So don't beat yourself up so much if on your tenth, or even hundredth, time in the synagogue you feel like a young child in Einstein's lab. This is normal, and most importantly, reading this book will help you learn exactly what you can do about it.

Let's Talk Some Shop

From our school years we can remember our parents and teachers telling us that proper preparation saves lots of perspiration. And as much as we hated to hear it, they were right. So, to make our

9

parents proud, we'll start at the beginning, and really become prepared for our next visit to the synagogue.

Let's start by defining prayer. Prayer is a big word, it carries a lot of "baggage." One person may conjure up an image of a servant and his master; another may think of prayer as something you do only when in trouble; a student might think back to the day of his college finals. But, what do we, as Jews, believe and know about prayer?

God: Pray to me

Prayer is a commandment of God. We are told to pray to Him for our needs, and in our prayers we often address God as our Merciful Father, or as our Father in Heaven, for God regards us, and we regard ourselves, as His children.

You may ask: Why do we have to pray to God for our needs? Doesn't God know our needs even better than we do ourselves? Is not God, by His very nature, good and kind, and always willing to do us good? After all, children do not "pray" to their parents to feed them, and clothe them, and protect them; why should we pray to our Heavenly Father for such things?

The answer to these questions is not hard to find after a little reflection. It has been amply explained by our wise Sages, including the great teacher and guide, Maimonides. He lived some 800 years ago and was one of the greatest codifiers of Jewish law. He wrote the following concerning prayer:

10

"We are told to offer up prayers to God, in order to establish firmly the true principle that God takes notice of our ways, that He can make them successful if we serve Him, or disastrous if we disobey Him; that success and failure are not the result of chance or accident." As is the case with all other commandments that God has given the Jewish people, the commandment to pray is not for His sake but for ours.

And you are right, God does not need our prayers; He can do without our prayers, but *we* cannot do without our prayers. It is good for *us* to acknowledge *our* dependence on God for our very life, our health, our daily bread, and our general welfare.

We do so every day, and many times a day. We need to remind ourselves that our life and happiness are a gift from our Creator, and in turn we try to be worthy of God's kindnesses and favors to us.

God does not owe us anything; yet He gives us everything. We should try to do the same for our fellow men and grant favors freely. We should express our gratitude to God not merely in words, but in deeds: By obeying His commands and living our daily life the way God wants us to – especially because it is all for our own good.

Knowing that God is good and that nothing is impossible for Him to do, we can go about our life with a deep sense of confidence and security. Even in times of distress we will not despair, knowing that in some way (best known to God) whatever happens to us is for our own good. It is a blessing in disguise.

11

Nevertheless, we pray to God to help us out of our distress, and grant us good that is not hidden or disguised. That He give us the good that is obvious even to humans who have limited under-standing.

We gain strength, courage and hope by trusting in God, and our daily prayers strengthen this trust in God. "In God We Trust" has been our Jewish motto since we first became a people.

Let's Go a Bit Deeper

The Hebrew word תפלה (*t'fillah*) is generally translated as "prayer," but this is not an accurate translation. To pray means to beg, beseech, implore, and the like, and we have a number of Hebrew words that more accurately convey this meaning. Our daily prayers are not merely requests to God to give us our daily needs and nothing more. Of course, such requests are also included in our prayers, but mostly our prayers are much more than that, as we shall see.

Going Up

Our Sages declare that the ladder which our forefather Jacob saw in his dream, with angels of God "going up and coming down," was also the symbol of prayer. Our Sages explain that by showing the ladder to Jacob in his dream, a ladder which "stood on the earth and reached into the heaven," God showed Jacob that prayer is like a ladder which connects the earth with the heaven, man with God.

The meaningful words of prayer, the good resolutions which it brings forth, are transformed into angels that go to God, Who then sends them down with blessings in return. That is why Jacob saw in his dream that angels were "going up and coming down," although one would have expected angels to first come down and *then* go up.

Thus, what we said about prayer in answer to the question: "Why do we pray?" is but the first step on the "ladder" of prayer. Prayer also has to do with things that are on a higher level than daily material needs — namely spiritual things.

A Time of Self-Judgment

The Hebrew word תפלה (*t'fillah*) comes from the verb פלל (*pallel*), "to judge." The reflexive verb להתפלל (*l'hitpallel*) "to pray" also means, "to judge oneself." Thus, the time of prayer is a time of self-judgment and self-evaluation.

When a person addresses himself to God and prays for His blessings, he must inevitably search his heart and examine whether he measures up to the standards of daily conduct which God has prescribed for man to follow. If he is honest with himself, he will be filled with humility, realizing that he hardly merits the blessings and favors for which he is asking. This is why we stress in our prayers God's infinite goodness and mercies. We pray to God to grant us our heart's desires, not because we merit them, but even though we may not deserve them.

13

This is also why our prayers, on weekdays, contain a confession of sins which we may have committed, knowingly or unknowingly. We pray for God's forgiveness, and resolve to better ourselves.

So we see how prayer can also help us lead a better life in every respect, by living more fully the way of the Torah and mitzvot, which God commanded us.

Jewish Customer Service

On an even higher level, prayer becomes עבודה *(avodah)*, "service." The Torah commands us "to serve God with our hearts," and our Sages say: "What kind of service is 'service of the heart?' – it is prayer." In this sense, prayer is meant to purify our hearts and our nature.

The plain Hebrew meaning of *avodah* is "work." We work with a raw material and convert it into a refined and finished product. In the process, we remove the impurities, or roughness, of the raw material, whether it is a piece of wood or a rough diamond, and make it into a thing of usefulness or beauty.

The tanner, for example, takes raw hide and converts it into fine leather. The parchment on which a Torah Scroll, a *Mezuzah*, or *Tefillin* is written, is made of the hide of a kosher animal. Raw wool full of grease and other impurities, through stages of "work," is made into fine wool, from which we can make not only fine clothes, but also a *Tallit* (prayer shawl), or *Tzitzit* (fringed garment).

Diamonds Are Forever

The Jewish people have been likened in the Torah to soil and earth, and have been called God's "land of desire." The saintly Ba'al Shem Tov, the founder of Chassidism, explained it this way: The earth is full of treasures, but they are often buried deep inside. It is necessary to dig for them; and when you discover them, you still have to clear away the impurities, refine them or polish them, as in the case of gold or diamonds.

Similarly, every Jew is full of wonderful treasures of character — modesty, kindness and other natural traits — but sometimes they are buried deep and covered up by "soil" and "dust," which have to be cleared away.

Define Refined

We speak of a person of good character as a "refined" person, or of "refined" character. It is often difficult to overcome such bad traits as pride, anger, jealousy, which may be quite "natural" but are still unbecoming for a human being, especially a Jew.

Tefillah, in the sense of *avodah*, is the "refinery" where the impurities of character are done away with. These bad character traits stem from the "animal" soul in man, and are "natural" to it. But we are endowed with a "Divine" soul, which is a spark of Godliness itself, and the treasure of all the wonderful qualities which make a man superior to an animal.

15

During proper prayer, our Divine soul speaks to God, and even the animal soul is filled with holiness. We realize that we stand before the Holy One, blessed be He, and the whole material world with all its pains and pleasures seems to melt away. We become aware of things that really matter and are truly important; even as we pray for life, health and sustenance, we think of these things in their deeper sense: a life that is worthy to be called "living"; health that is not only physical, but above all spiritual; sustenance – the things that truly sustain us in this world and in the world to come – the Torah and mitzvot.

We feel cleansed and purified by such "service," and when we return to our daily routine, the feeling of purity and holiness lingers and raises our daily conduct to a level fitting for a member of the people called a "kingdom of priests and a holy nation."

Attached to God

The highest level on the "ladder" of prayer is reached when we are so inspired as to want nothing but the feeling of attachment with God. On this level *tefillah* is related to the verb (used in Mishnaic Hebrew) תופל *(tofel)*, to "attach," "join," or "bind together," as two pieces of a broken vessel are pieced together to make it whole again.

Our soul is truly a part of God, and therefore longs to be reunited with, and reabsorbed in, Godliness, just as a small flame when it is put close to a larger flame, is absorbed into the larger flame. We may not be aware of this longing, but it is there nonetheless.

Our soul has, in fact, been called the "candle of God." The flame of a candle is restless, striving upwards, to break away, as it were, from the wick and body of the candle; for such is the nature of fire — to strive upwards. Our soul, too, strives upwards, like that flame. This is also one of the reasons why a Jew naturally sways while praying. For prayer is the means whereby we attach ourselves to God, with a soulful attachment of "spirit to spirit," and in doing so our soul flutters and soars upward, to be united with God.

Mitzvah Bar

Let us examine this idea more closely. Every mitzvah which God has commanded us to do, and which we perform as a sacred commandment, attaches us to God. The word mitzvah is related to the Aramaic word צוותא (*tzavta*), "togetherness," or "company." In English, too, we have the verb "to enjoin," which means "to command," for the commandment is the bond that joins together the person commanded with the person commanding, no matter how far apart they may be in distance, rank or position.

When a king commands a humble servant to do something, this establishes a bond between the two. The humble servant feels greatly honored that the king has taken notice of him and has given him something to do, and that he, an insignificant person, can do something to please the great king. It makes him eager to be worthy of the king's attention and favor. If this is so in the case of every mitzvah, it is even more so in the case of prayer. For nothing brings

17

us closer to God than prayer, when it is truly the outpouring of the soul and, therefore, makes for an "attachment of spirit to spirit," as mentioned earlier. If any mitzvah brings us closer to God, prayer (on the level we are speaking) is like being embraced by God. There is no greater pleasure or fulfillment than the wonderful spiritual uplift and blissfulness resulting from prayer.

Prose that Rose

Prayer, we said, is like a "ladder" of many rungs. To get to the top of it, we must start at the bottom and steadily rise upwards. To enable us to do so, our prayers have been composed prophetically by our saintly Prophets and Sages of old, and have been ordered also like a "ladder," steadily leading us to greater and greater inspiration. We must, therefore, become familiar with our prayers: first of all their plain meaning, then their deeper meaning, and finally the whole "order" of the service.

The Three Daily Prayers

Jewish Law requires us to pray three times daily: Morning, afternoon and evening. These prayers are called *Shacharit* (morning prayer), *Minchah* (afternoon prayer) and *Arvit*, or *Maariv* (evening prayer). Our Sages tell us that our Patriarchs, Abraham, Isaac and Jacob originally introduced the custom of praying three times a day. Abraham introduced prayer in the morning; Isaac instituted afternoon prayer, and Jacob added one at night.

In the *Zohar* (or *kabbalah*, the mystical part of the Torah) it is explained further that each of the three Patriarchs represented a particular quality which they introduced into the service of God. Abraham served God with love; Isaac with awe; and Jacob with mercy. Not that each lacked the qualities of the others, but each had a particular quality that was more prominent.

Thus Abraham distinguished himself especially in the quality of kindness (חסד) and love (אהבה), while Isaac excelled especially in the quality of strict justice (דין) and reverence (יראה), while Jacob inherited both these qualities, bringing out a new quality which combined the first two into the well-balanced and lasting quality of truth (אמת) and mercy (רחמים).

We, the children of Abraham, Isaac and Jacob, have inherited all three great qualities of our Patriarchs, enabling us to serve God and pray to Him with love, fear (awe) and mercy. The quality of mercy comes in when we realize that our soul is a part of Godliness, and we feel pity for it because it is so often distracted from God by the material aspects of daily life.

Life's Big Instruction Book

When the Torah was given to us at Mount Sinai, our way of life was set out for us by God. Torah means "teaching," "instruction," "guidance"; for the Torah teaches us our way of living, including every detail of our daily life.

19

The Torah contains 613 commandments. Among them is the command to "serve God with all our heart and all our soul." By praying to Him we fulfill not only the commandment of prayer, but also other commandments, such as to love God and to fear Him.

During the first one thousand years or so from the time of Moshe *Rabbeinu* (Moses), there was no set order of prayer. Each individual was duty-bound to pray to God every day, but the form of prayer was left to the individual.

There was, however, a set order of service in the *Beit Hamikdash* (the Holy Temple that stood in Jerusalem) in connection with the daily sacrifices, morning and afternoon, with the latter sacrifice extending into the night. On special days, such as Shabbat, *Rosh Chodesh* (start of a new month) and Festivals, there were also "additional" (*musaf*) sacrifices.

Accordingly, it was not unusual for some Jews to pray three times a day – morning, afternoon, and evening – in their own way. King David, for example, declared that he prayed three times daily, and Daniel (in Babylon) prayed three times daily facing the direction of Jerusalem. There is evidence that even during the time of the first *Beit Hamikdash*, there were public places of prayer, called *Beit Ha-am*, which the Chaldeans (Babylonians) destroyed, along with the *Beit Hamikdash* and the rest of Jerusalem.

Prayer for Beginners

After the *Beit Hamikdash* was destroyed and the Jews were led into captivity in Babylon, Jews continued to gather and pray in congregation. The places of prayer became like "small sanctuaries." But during the years of exile, the children that were born and raised in Babylon lacked adequate knowledge of the Holy Tongue, Hebrew, and spoke a mixed language.

Therefore, when the Jews returned to their homeland after the seventy years of exile were over, Ezra the Scribe together with the Men of the Great Assembly (consisting of Prophets and Sages, 120 members in all) set the text of the daily prayer, *Shemoneh Esrei* – the "Eighteen Benedictions", and made it a permanent institution and duty in Jewish life to recite this prayer three times daily.

Ever since then it became part of Jewish Law (*halacha*) for each and every Jew to pray this ordained and fixed order of prayer three times daily, corresponding to the daily sacrifices in the *Beit Hamikdash*, with additional (*Musaf*) prayers on Shabbat, Rosh Chodesh and Festivals, and a special "closing" prayer (*Neilah*) on Yom Kippur.

Thus, the main parts of the daily prayers were formulated by our Sages, are still the main parts of our morning and evening prayers.

The *Shema* was included in the morning and evening prayers, and the daily Psalm, which used to be sung by the Levites in the *Beit*

Hamikdash, became part of the morning prayer. Other Psalms of David were included in the morning prayer, and special benedictions before and after the *Shema* were added. By the time the Mishna was recorded by Rabbi Judah the Prince about the year 3,910 (some 500 years after Ezra; 150 C.E.), and especially by the time the Talmud was completed (some 300 years later, or about 1500 years ago), the basic order of our prayers, as we know them now, had been formulated.

The Recipe

The morning service consists of the following sections:
1) The blessings upon rising from bed, 2) The chapters of praise,
3) The blessings for the *Shema*, 4) The *Shema*, 5) The *Amidah*, and
6) The concluding prayers.

1) Upon waking in the morning we express our gratitude to God for the rest we had, for giving us back all our senses and restoring strength to our weary limbs. We thank God also for the great privilege of being a Jew and serving God, for having given us His holy Torah, and so on.

2) Then we recite Psalms of praise to God, describing His majesty and might, as the Creator of Heaven and Earth and all creatures, His loving-kindness and goodness in taking care of all creatures.

3-4) Having thus been inspired by God's goodness and love, we declare the Unity of God, and we take upon ourselves to love God and observe all His commands.

5) After all the above, we come to the main part of the prayer — the *Amidah*, in which we put our requests before God.

6) We then conclude the service with appropriate Psalms and prayers.

This is again one of the reasons why prayer has been likened to a ladder ("Jacob's Ladder") connecting earth and heaven. For the sections of our prayer indeed are like the rungs of a ladder, one leading to the other.

Shmoozing with God

So, as we see from the above, prayer time in the synagogue is too valuable to blow on shmooz, news, and maybe even a little snooze. It is a sacred time of real communion with God, a time of self-analysis and self-growth.

Think of it as being invited to participate in an intricate experiment in a laboratory, or given a chance to take part in exciting activities on the trading floor of the Stock Exchange, or for that matter, an opportunity to change things in your own life, and instead we sit there lounging with a newspaper or making small talk, all while this great stuff is happening all around us.

So, we are indeed ready to give 60 or 90 minutes of our attention to the matter at hand in the synagogue and leave the socializing for the golf course, or Sundays, or the Kiddush that usually follows the services on Shabbat.

23

But, you may ask, what do we do then with all this "new" free time? And how do I "turn on" this mystic connection with God?

Enter the Prayer Book

For many years during the period of the Holy Temple (some 2,000 years ago), the Jewish people prayed by heart. As times changed, and younger generations were not learning the prayers, it was time to set them in fixed order in a book. This book was called a *Siddur*. The Siddur became our traditional prayer book, containing the three daily prayers, and the prayers for Shabbat, Rosh Chodesh and the Festivals.

"Siddur" means "order," since in the Siddur we find our prayers in their proper and fixed order. Sometimes, for the sake of convenience, the Shabbat and Rosh Chodesh prayers may be printed in a separate volume. The prayers for Rosh Hashanah and Yom Kippur are usually printed in separate volumes, called *Machzor* ("cycle"). Sometimes the prayers for the Three Festivals – Pesach, Shavuot and Sukkot – are also printed in separate volumes.

The oldest Siddur that we know of is the Siddur of Rav *Amram Gaon*, Head of the Yeshiva of Sura, in Babylon, about 1,100 years ago. He had prepared it at the request of the Jews of Barcelona, Spain. It contains the arrangements of the prayers for the entire year, including also some laws concerning prayer and customs. It was copied and used by the Jews of France and Germany, and was in fact the standard prayer book for all Jewish communities.

The *Seder Rav Amram Gaon* remained in handwritten form for about 1,000 years, until it was printed for the first time in Warsaw in 1865.

Rav *Saadia Gaon*, who was head of the Sura Yeshiva less than 100 years after Rav Amram Gaon, arranged a Siddur for the Jews in Arab countries, with explanations and instructions in Arabic. The *Rambam*, Maimonides, also prepared the order of the prayers for the whole year (including the Haggadah of Pesach), and included it in his famous Code of Jewish Law, following the section dealing with the laws of prayer.

The structure of the prayers remains basically the same. The morning prayers begin with the morning blessings, continue with *Pesukei D'zimra* (Psalms and sections from the Prophets, introduced and concluded by benedictions), followed by the *Shema* (which is also introduced and concluded by benedictions), and continues with the main prayer, *Shemoneh Esrei*, which means "eighteen," because originally this prayer had eighteen blessings (in the weekday version), and is also known as the *Amidah* ("standing"), because it must be recited in a standing position.

101 Ways to Tell God "I Love You"

So, the Siddur is our "code book," with all the necessary words proven to kindle within us the whole gamut of feelings we need to feel. And the early rabbis did us the greatest favor by putting it all in order.

Suppose you were at a high school reunion, and were suddenly asked to stand up and make a speech about your memories, feelings, perhaps some wishes you had, all in front of a familiar but now estranged crowd. Wouldn't it be easier if you had some outline to get you started?

This is the value of the prayers, their outline, order and sequence, down to the words and letters chosen. They help us experience the befitting emotion.

I know we may not all be poets, but it is really difficult to read through the prayers and *not* feel moved at some point or another to the appropriate feelings. At one time it will be one prayer that does it. Another time a different one. But the goal is always the same.

Feel God, thank God, appreciate what we've got, and ask God to give us strength to pull through for Him, for ourselves, and for the entire Jewish people.

Blast the Rote to Heaven

It is easy, after a while, to read familiar prayers too quickly, or without real concentration. It can become a habit. Yet familiarity need not necessarily make it so, for as we know — people eat three times a day, and usually enjoy every meal. So when we pray and give our prayer a little thought, we can find great inspiration and uplift in them. At least, on the day of Shabbat and Festivals, when we have less to worry about, we can pray with even greater devotion.

A Quick Prayer Primer

The first thing that is essential is at least to know the meaning and translation of the words of the prayers. If we cannot concentrate every day on the entire prayers, it would be a good idea one day to concentrate on one part, the next day on the next part, so that in the course of a week we will have concentrated on all the prayers. Or to make Shabbat or Holiday the special day on which to work through the prayers like a real mystic.

To get you started, we help guide you through the High-Holiday prayer book with simple guides to each page. We have also included English transliterations of key prayers, to assist those to whom the Hebrew language is not yet familiar to read or sing along in the original Hebrew.

It is recommended that you keep this book with you during the services and refer to it before each prayer. It will boost the octane of your experience.

Please note: Since one of the prohibited actions on the Shabbat and Yom Kippur is carrying items from a private domain into a public one and vice versa, make sure to bring this book to the synagogue before the onset of Shabbat or Yom Kippur. Alternatively, you can use it during the week as a study guide in its own right.

Rosh Hashana

What is Rosh Hashanah?

"The first day of the seventh month [Tishrei] shall be a sacred holiday to you when you may not do any mundane work. It shall be a day of sounding the (ram's) horn." (Num. 29: 1)

Rosh Hashanah is the anniversary of the day on which God completed the creation of this world by creating Adam, the first man. Adam's very first act was to proclaim the Almighty as King of the Universe. He called upon all creatures: "Come, let us worship, bow down, and kneel before God, our maker."

Each Rosh Hashanah, we too proclaim the Kingship of God, and reaffirm our commitment to serve Him well.

Just as on the original Rosh Hashanah, God created the world for the first time, so on each Rosh Hashanah He reconsiders and re-evaluates the quality of our relationship with Him, and creates our world anew.

The Holiday of Rosh Hashanah stirs the heart of every Jew. The Jewish New Year is a time of awe and solemnity. On this day we re-establish and intensify our relationship with God and are judged, together with all of mankind, as to the events of the coming year.

Throughout Rosh Hashanah, we are attuned to the holiness of the day. All our activities — praying in the synagogue, listening to the shofar, and partaking of festive meals — are imbued with an awareness of God's Kingship.

On Rosh Hashanah we stand before the Almighty, united with Jews everywhere, and pray for a year of health, prosperity and peace. The words we read in the *Machzor*, the special holiday prayer book, help us channel our thoughts and prayers upward, shaped by the stirring and incisive words of our great Sages. Our hearts are awakened to the awesome power of the day.

Rosh Hashanah means "head of the year." Just as the head controls the entire body, so does Rosh Hashanah contain within it the potential for life, blessing and sustenance for the entire year. Our actions on Rosh Hashanah set the tone for the year to come. For this reason we are careful in all we think, say and do during these two days.

We pray that God, in turn, will grant us a good and sweet year. Our wishes for one another are reflected in the words which we say after services on the first night of Rosh Hashanah, *L'shanah tovah tikateiv v'teichatem*: "May you be written and inscribed for a good year."

The Rosh Hashanah Services

When	What	Page in Holiday Prayer Book*
Rosh Hashanah Eve	Candle Lighting	22
	Evening Service	28-44 23-44 – When Rosh Hashanah begins on Friday night.
Rosh Hashanah Day	Morning Service	66-264
	Torah Reading	160
	Shofar Service	175
	Musaf Service	177
	Priestly Blessing	218
Rosh Hashanah Afternoon	Afternoon Service	267-290
	Tashlich Prayer	291

* Kehot Hebrew/English *Machzor* for Rosh Hashanah Annotated Edition

Prayer for Welcoming the Shabbat

Prayerbook Pages 23 through 27

When Rosh Hashanah falls on the Shabbat, the services begin with special prayers for welcoming the Shabbat, known as *Kabbalat Shabbat*. These prayers start on top of page 23 and continue through page 28 in the High Holiday prayer book. They are usually recited while standing.

Page 23 (TR: 111): *Mizmor L'dovid* (**A Psalm by David**). This Psalm, recited while standing, inaugurates the Shabbat. The seven repetitions of the words *kol hashem* ("Voice of the Lord") in this Psalm correspond to the seven days of Creation, when everything was created by God's word.

Page 24 (TR: 111): *Lecho Dodi* (**Come, my Beloved**). This beautiful hymn, welcoming the Shabbat Queen, is recited while standing. After each paragraph we repeat the verse *L'cho Dodi*.

The refrain of this hymn *L'cho Dodi* and, indeed, the entire motif of the hymn, in which the Shabbat is represented as a "Queen" whom we go out to welcome, is based on a Talmudic source, where we are told how two great Sages welcomed the Shabbat. Rabbi Chanina used to dress himself in honor of Shabbat and say (to his disciples): "Come, let us go out to welcome the Shabbat Queen." Rabbi Yannai, dressed in his Shabbat clothes, would announce: "*Bo-i Chalo, Bo-i Chalo*" — Come in, Bride; come in, Bride.

 Page 26 (TR: 155): **Mourner's Kaddish.** At specifically marked intervals during the prayers, when praying with a quorum of at least ten Jewish male adults, mourners recite this Kaddish. All rise for this Kaddish.

Kaddish means "holy." It was composed, like most of our prayers, by the *Anshay K'nesset Hagedolah* — the Men of the Great Assembly. It is based on the wording of Ezekiel's prophecy in which *Kiddush Hashem*, the sanctification of God's Name, is placed in the center of the national duty of Israel, upon which the deliverance of the Jewish nation was dependent. The *Amen* that the congregation responds, is like the word *Emunah*, which means belief, and by stating it we acknowledge that we believe what the reader has stated.

The Rosh Hashanah Evening Service

Prayerbook Pages 28 through 44

The evening service consists of the following segments:

1. Half Kaddish and *Bor'chu*.

2. The *Shema*.

3. The *Amidah*.

4. Concluding prayers.

When Rosh Hashanah falls on Shabbat, the services begin at the top of page 23 in the High Holiday prayer book.

Page 28 (TR: 113): **Half Kaddish and *Bor'chu* (Bless).** The leader recites Half Kaddish followed by *Bor'chu*. The prayer of *Bor'chu* is a summons, or call, by the leader to join him in praising God. It is explained in the *Zohar* or *Kabbalah*, that all mitzvot require proper preparation; we do not want to perform the sacred mitzvot like robots, without proper mental preparation. We want to pause to think of the great significance of the mitzvah we are about to perform.

This same benediction is said once again at the end of the Shabbat evening prayer, for those who may have tarried in coming to the synagogue (they were occupied preparing for the Shabbat) and have not heard its first recital.

Bor'chu is recited standing, and with a special bow of the head in reverence to the One and Only God. After *Bor'chu* we may be seated.

Page 30 (TR: 113): **The *Shema* (Hear, O Israel).** The *Shema*, the essence of our faith, is recited at this point. It is customary to cover our eyes with our right hand while reciting the first verse of the *Shema*, to promote deep concentration.

The *Shema* consists of three chapters taken from the Bible. The first chapter begins with the proclamation: "Hear, O Israel, the Lord is our God, the Lord is One." It goes on to tell us that we must love God and dedicate our lives to the carrying out of His will. We can keep this faith alive only if we bring up our children in this belief. This section also contains the two mitzvot of *tefillin* and *mezuzah*, which remind us that we are Jews.

The second chapter contains a promise that if we carry out God's commands we shall be a happy people in our land. If not, we will suffer exile and hardships in strange lands, so that by suffering and trouble we will learn the ways of God and return to Him. We are again reminded to teach our children our true faith, and the *tefillin* and *mezuzah* are again mentioned, being the symbols of practical observance of God's commands.

The third chapter contains the commandment of *tzitzit*, the distinctive Jewish garment which is a constant reminder of all the precepts of the Torah. We are also reminded that God brought us out of Egypt and made us His people, and that we accepted Him as our God.

Page 33: The *Amidah*. We rise for the *Amidah*, the prayer in which we put forth our requests to God, and the leader first recites Half Kaddish.

Before beginning the *Amidah*, we take three steps back, and then three steps forward, as if approaching a King.

[It is important to note that when Rosh Hashanah occurs on Shabbat, we include the special portions marked for the Shabbat in the *Amidah.*]

The *Amidah* is concluded by taking three steps back, as if departing from the presence of a King, at the verse *Oseh Ha-shalom* (He who makes the peace) on page 34, and three steps forward after completing the sentence.

Page 39: Shabbat Additions. When Rosh Hashanah occurs on Shabbat, we continue with *Va-y'chulu* (The heavens), in the middle of page 34, and *Mogayn Ovos* (He was a shield); we stand for these prayers. Otherwise, we continue with *L'dovid Mizmor* (By David, a Psalm), in the middle of page 40.

Va-y'chulu (TR: 113). By reciting *Va-y'chulu*, a Jew gives testimony that God created the heavens and the earth, and all that is in them, in six days, and rested on the seventh day, which He proclaimed a holy day of rest. The Jewish people are the living witnesses that attest to this truth, and every Jew should realize the great and unique privilege to be such a witness. Hence the *Zohar* concludes: "A Jew should give this testimony with joy and gladness of heart."

Mogayn Ovos (TR: 114). The words "He was a shield," "He resurrects the dead" and "the holy King" clearly refer to the familiar first three blessings of the *Amidah.* The words "for to them He decided to give rest" refer to the central Shabbat blessing *r'tzay vim'nuchosaynu,* "please find favor in our rest."

37

The words "We will serve Him," "God worthy of praise" and "Master of Peace" refer to the familiar last three blessings of every Amidah.

Page 40 (TR: 114): *L'dovid Mizmor* (By David, a Psalm). The leader recites this Psalm, and we repeat it after him, line by line.

This Psalm is dedicated to the kingship of God. With the creation of man, God became King, for one cannot be a king if he has no subjects to rule. Adam became God's first subject and he immediately proclaimed the sovereignty of the Creator: "King of the Universe."

For this reason this Psalm has been made an important part of the High Holiday prayers. For Rosh Hashanah, as we all know, is the anniversary of the creation of man, and of the "Coronation" of the King of kings.

Page 40 (TR: 115): **Whole Kaddish and *Olaynu* (It is incumbent upon us).** We remain standing, and the leader recites Whole Kaddish. Then we proceed with the concluding prayer, *Olaynu*.

The famous Rav Hai Gaon, the last of the Babylonian Geonim, states that the prayer of *Olaynu* was composed by Joshua as he led the children of Israel into the Promised Land. (The initials taken from the first letter of each sentence in the first paragraph, read backwards, form his name "Hoshea.") Thus, when Joshua was about to settle the Jewish people in the Holy Land, he made them remember, through this hymn, that they were different from the Canaanite peoples and other nations and tribes of the earth, who "worship vain things and emptiness."

[When Rosh Hashanah falls on Shabbat, before *Olaynu* we recite *Mizmor L'dovid* (A Psalm by David), Half Kaddish and *Bor'chu* (Bless).]

Page 43 (TR: 155): **Mourner's Kaddish.** Remain standing for the Mourner's Kaddish (recited only when at least ten adult Jewish males are praying).

Page 44 (TR: 116): **Greeting for Rosh Hashanah.** It is customary on the first night of Rosh Hashanah to greet one another with this special greeting.

The Rosh Hashanah Morning Service

 Prayerbook Pages 79 through 264

The morning service consists of the following segments:

1. The morning prayers.

2. The *Shema.*

3. The *Amidah.*

39

4. The reading of the Torah.

5. The Shofar service.

6. The *Musaf* service.

7. The priestly blessing.

Page 78 (TR: 155): **Mourner's Kaddish and *Hodu* (Offer praise).** The Mourner's Kaddish is recited standing. We then begin *Hodu*, which can be recited while sitting.

The opening prayers are mostly devoted to the expression of thanks for God's help and grace. The first part of *Hodu* comes from the first book of Chronicles. King David composed this prayer, and the famous singer Asaph and his choir sang it in the Sanctuary on the day when the Holy Ark was returned to Jerusalem.

The second section, which begins with *Shiru La-shem* (Sing to the Lord) and ends with *V'hallel La-shem* (and praise to the Lord), was said in the Temple every evening, right after the completion of the offerings. It pictures the future as promised to us in the holy Scriptures, when God will be recognized by all of mankind, and Israel will be respected as the true servants of God.

Page 81: *Hashem Melech* **(The Lord is King) and Psalms.** At this point the congregation rises to recite *Hashem Melech*, which is near the bottom of the page. When this is completed, we may sit down and continue the Psalms with *Lam'na-tzayach* (For the choirmaster). The central theme of these passages is God's reign upon all the earth. Thus, while we recognize our good fortune in that God has been especially gracious to us in bringing us close to Him, we hope and pray for the day when all the nations of the world will also acknowledge God and fear Him.

Page 87 (TR: 116-118): *Hallelukah* (Praise the Lord), *Hodu La-shem Ki Tov* (Praise the Lord), and *Hoaderes* (Power). We rise for the Psalm *Hallelukah*, at the top of the page.

Our Sages explain that the 26 verses of praise to God in *Hodu La-shem Ki Tov* allude to the 26 generations of the human race that preceded the giving of the Torah at Mt. Sinai. Since the world was created for the sake of the Torah, and without Torah it could not have existed on its own merits, the world was sustained during this period entirely by God's boundless kindness. The 26 generations (2448 years) comprise the ten generations from Adam to Noah; another ten from Noah to Abraham; and the next six generations, namely, Isaac, Jacob, Levi, Kehot, Amram and Moses.

Pages 89 (TR: 119): *Boruch She-omar* (Blessed is He who spoke). Men gather the front two fringes of their prayer-shawl or *tzitzit*, and hold them in their right hand. Then the two paragraphs, *L'shaym* (For the sake) and *Boruch She-omar*, are recited. Afterwards, the fringes are kissed and released. We may be seated.

Page 91 (TR: 120): *Ashray* (Happy are those) and Songs of **Praise.** The Psalm of *Ashray*, in the middle of page 91, introduces a series of songs of praise, written by King David. We take a closer look at the beautiful world we live in and offer praise to its Maker.

Pages 95-100: *Boruch* (Blessed). Rise for Boruch, a set of prayers recounting our exodus from Egypt and praising God for His deliverance. Remain standing until after *Bor'chu* (Bless), near the top of page 101.

Pages 100-103 (TR: 121, 113, 122): *Uv'Chayn* Y*ishtabach,* (And therefore), *Shir Ha-ma-alos* (A Song of Ascents), Half Kaddish, Bor'chu (Bless), and *Kel Adon* (Almighty God). The leader recites *Shir Ha-ma-alos*, followed by Half Kaddish and *Bor'chu*, a call to prayer. After *Bor'chu* we may be seated. When Rosh Hashanah occurs on the Shabbat, we continue with the prayers under the heading, "On Shabbat". Otherwise, continue with the section, "On weekdays".

Pages 105-107 (TR: 113): **The** *Shema* (Hear, O Israel). In preparation for the *Shema*, while reciting the words *Va-havi-aynu L'sholom* (Bring us in peace), in the middle of the page, men gather all four fringes of their prayer-shawl or *tzitzit*. The *tzitzit* are held until *Lo-ad Ka-yemet* (abide forever), in the middle of page 107.

The *Shema*, the essence of our faith, is then recited. It is customary to cover our eyes with our right hand while reciting the first verse of the *Shema*, to promote deep concentration. While reciting the portion of the *tzitzit*, each time we say the word *tzitzit*, we bring the tzitzit to our lips, and give them a kiss. This shows our deep reverence and love for this commandment.

Pages 109-114: The Amidah. We rise for the *Amidah*, the prayer in which we put forth our requests to God, begins on the bottom of page 109 and continues through page 114. Before beginning the *Amidah*, we take three steps back, and then three steps forward, as if approaching a King. When Rosh Hashanah occurs on Shabbat, we include the special portions marked for the Shabbat in the *Amidah*.

The *Amidah* is concluded by taking three steps back, as if departing from the presence of a King, at the verse *Oseh Ha-shalom* (He who makes the peace) on bottom of page 114, and three steps forward after completing the sentence.

Pages 115-152: The Leader's Repetition of the *Amidah*. The repetition of the *Amidah* is recited by the leader. At various points during the repetition, the congregation participates by reading the portions marked "Congregation." There are different readings for the first and second days of Rosh Hashanah. As a rule, we stand whenever the ark is opened.

Page 126 (TR: 124): *L'kayl Orayeh Din* (To the Almighty who arranges judgment). This prayer continues in the spirit of praising God. In it we cite numerous examples of God's infinite loving-kindness. Note how this prayer is written in alphabetical order (the second letter of each verse proceeding in the order of the Hebrew alphabet).

Page 126 (TR: 123): *Kedusha.* Rise for *Nakdishoch* (We will hallow) at the bottom of the page. Here, the congregation recites one verse at a time, followed by the leader.

There is a great deal of preparation going on among the angelic hosts before they utter their prayers to sanctify their Creator: *Kadosh, kadosh, kadosh* (Holy, holy, holy). *Kadosh* also means "separate"; to say that "God is holy" is to say that God is separated from, and unaffected by, the world He created.

The repetition of the word "holy" three times is explained in the Aramaic translation of the *Kedusha* in the prayer of *Uva L'tzion*: "Holy in the heavens above, the abode of His glory; holy on earth, the work of His might; holy forever and ever."

While reciting this prayer, we stand with our feet together and refrain from any interruption. Afterwards we may be seated.

Page 130 (TR: 124-125): *Modim D'rabbonon* **(We thankfully acknowledge) and *Uch'sov* (Inscribe).** Rise for *Modim*, in the middle of the page. Recite this along with the leader's recitation.

Uch'sov. When the leader reaches *Uch'sov* (Inscribe), we recite this verse.

Page 132 (TR: 125): *Uv'sayfer Cha-yim* **(And in the Book of Life) and *Ovinu Malkaynu* (Our Father, our King).** When the leader reaches *Uv'sayfer Cha-yim*, we recite this verse with him.

When Rosh Hashanah falls during the week we recite the special prayer *Ovinu Malkaynu*. This prayer is said to have been recited by Rabbi Akiva during a drought in Jerusalem, and it was the only prayer that brought rain. So, too, when we request God's mercy for our own needs, we recite this same prayer. The ark is opened, and the congregation stands. This is followed by the recitation of the Whole Kaddish by the leader.

Pages 155-160 (TR: 155): **The Song of the Day and Mourner's Kaddish.** Locate and recite the Psalm that corresponds to this day of the week. It is then followed by the Mourner's Kaddish when a quorum of at least ten Jewish male adults are praying. All rise for this Kaddish.

In the days of old, when the *Beit Hamikdash* (Holy Temple) was in existence, the *Leviim* (Levites) had an important part in the holy

45

service conducted there daily. Their task was to sing hymns of praise to God, which they also accompanied on musical instruments. One of the highlights of the service of the Levites was the singing of the "Song of the Day." It consisted of a special Psalm from the Book of *Tehillim* (Psalms), a different one for each of the seven days of the week. This has been made part of our morning service.

The Rosh Hashanah Torah Reading

 Prayerbook Pages 160 through 174]

The Torah reading consists of the following segments:

1. Opening the Ark and bringing the Torah scrolls to the *bima* (reading table).

2. Reading from the first Torah.

3. Reading from the second Torah.

4. The Haftorah.

Page 160 (TR: 125): **Opening of the Ark and** *Va-y'hi Bin'soah* **(Whenever the Ark set out).** The ark is opened, and the Torah scrolls are taken to the reading table, from which the reader will read the portion for this day.

At this point we recite *Va-y'hi Bin'soah*, *Hashem, Hashem* (Lord, Lord), and a personal request of God, *Ribono Shel Olom* (Master of the world).

Va-y'hi Bin'soah: We bless God for having given us the Torah "with His holiness." The Torah and holiness are bound together. A holy way of life is one in which everything we do is dedicated to God. It is not a life of ease, but a life of service. God requires His people to be a "holy nation."

The Torah stresses: "You shall be holy; for I, your God, am holy." Thus, in the few words that comprise this short prayer, we bring up the past — Moses and the Ark; and the future — the day when all the earth will be filled with the knowledge of God. And the two are linked to the present — our dedication to the Torah in our present-day life.

Hashem, Hashem: We say this verse three times. The Thirteen Attributes of Mercy were revealed to Moses when he prayed for God's forgiveness for the sin of the Golden Calf. Our Sages say that on that occasion God, as it were, wrapped Himself in a *tallit*, like a leader stepping before the Ark, and said to Moses, "Thus shall you pray, saying, '*Hashem, Hashem....*'"

Thus, God showed to Moses how Jews can obtain God's forgiveness through *teshuvah* (repentance and return to God) and reciting the Thirteen Attributes of God's Mercy. For this reason, the Thirteen Attributes are recited during the High Holidays.

47

Page 162 (TR: 126): **The *Shema* (Hear).** While the Torah scrolls are held, the leader recites the verse of *Shema* (Hear), and *Echod* (Our God is One). We repeat each verse after him.

The leader then recites *Gad'lu* (Exalt), and we follow with *L'cho Hashem* (Lord, yours is the greatness), as the Torah scrolls are carried to the reading table.

When the Torah is taken from the Ark, it is a most appropriate time to declare our faith in the One God, for the Torah is also one and only, holy and eternal. The fact that the leader, who is our representative, makes this declaration while holding the Torah, and that we repeat it after him, is like declaring it on oath.

Pages 164-173: The Torah Reading. The Torah portions for the first and second days of Rosh Hashanah are found here.

The Torah Reading for the First Day

The birth of Isaac is the theme of the reading of the Torah on the first day of Rosh Hashanah. The portion contains a number of lessons. First, there is the lesson of Divine Providence and Omnipotence. Sarah, at the age of ninety, gives birth to her first and only child, Isaac, when Abraham is one hundred years old. Isaac is entered into the Covenant of our father Abraham at the age of eight days, as God has commanded.

The importance of upbringing and education is also emphasized in this portion. Seeing that Ishmael, Isaac's elder half-brother, the son of Hagar, exercises a bad influence on the younger Isaac, Sarah insists on sending away both Hagar and her son. Lost in the desert of

Beer-Sheva and on the brink of a painful death from thirst, Divine Providence saves Ishmael by a miraculous revelation of a well.

The portion concludes with an episode illustrating Abraham's rise in the eyes of the surrounding neighbors, when Abimelech, king of the Philistines, comes to visit Abraham to conclude a covenant of peace with him.

❖⋗✲⋖❖

The Torah Reading for the Second Day

On the second day of Rosh Hashanah, the "Binding of Isaac" (*Akeidat Yitzchok*) is the theme of the reading in the Torah, which directly follows the portion of the previous day. It is the symbol of self-sacrifice with which we, the children of Abraham, are always ready to obey God's commands, and for which God has promised us His blessings.

49

 **Page 169** (TR: 127): **Lifting of the First Torah, and Reading from the Second Torah.** With the conclusion of the reading from the first Torah, the Torah is lifted for all to see, and we recite *V'zos Ha-toroh* (This is the Torah). This is the same Torah which Moses placed before the children of Israel. Nothing in it has changed. It is as relevant today as it was then.

The second Torah is set on the reading table, and the portion of the Torah in which God commands us regarding the observances of Rosh Hashanah is read.

Lifting of the Second Torah: As the Torah is lifted, we once again proclaim, *V'zos Ha-toroh* (This is the Torah).

The Haftorah. The Haftorah, a selection from the Prophets, is read. There is a special Haftorah for each of the two days of Rosh Hashanah.

✦⊱✿⊰✦

The Haftorah for the First Day

The birth of Samuel is the theme of the Haftorah. Both Sarah and Hannah had been childless and barren, but God eventually blessed them each with a son. Both Isaac and Samuel were consecrated to the service of God: Isaac through the Akedah (Binding), and Samuel as a prophet. The Haftorah concludes with the significant words: "Those

50

who contend with the Lord will be crushed, He will thunder against them in heaven; the Lord will judge the furthest corners of the earth, give strength to His king, and raise the glory of His anointed one." Here the prophetess Hannah refers to the final Day of Judgment and the "horn of His anointed one" — a theme which we mention many times in our prayers of this day.

✦ ≒✦✷✦≔ ✦

The Haftorah for the Second Day

The Haftorah suitably speaks of the final rebuilding and redemption of Israel: "For the Lord will redeem Jacob, and deliver him from a power mightier than he....Thus said the Lord: Keep your voice from weeping, your eyes from tears, for there is a reward for your deeds...they shall return from the land of the enemy....There is hope for your future...the children shall return to their border."

The Haftorah concludes with God's moving declaration of His everlasting love and mercy for Israel: "Is Ephraim not My beloved son, is he not a precious child that whenever I speak of him I recall him even more?....I will surely have compassion on him, declares the Lord."

Pages 174: *Y'kum Purkon* (**May there come forth**). When Rosh Hashanah falls on the Shabbat, after the Haftorah is completed we recite *Y'kum Purkon*.

The Shofar Service

 ## Prayerbook Pages 175 through 178]

The Shofar service consists of the following segments:

1. Preparatory Psalms.

2. Blessing over the mitzvah.

3. The sounding of the shofar.

4. Concluding verses.

The primary mitzvah and central theme of Rosh Hashanah is the blowing of the shofar. As Maimonides puts it, the shofar says to every individual, "Wake up from your sleep!"

Even a highly spiritual person must take to heart the call of the shofar. Compared to the level that each of us is capable of reaching, there is still much room for improvement. When the Jewish people hear the shofar, their hearts are opened, they shudder over their sins, and in a brief moment their reflections turn to repentance. We can and must effect an inner change – one so radical that our previous existence will seem to us as though we had been in a deep sleep.

The Shofar service is not performed when Rosh Hashanah occurs on the Shabbat.

Page 175 (TR: 127): **Preparatory Psalms and *Lam'natzayach* (To the choirmaster).** We rise and remain standing through the *Musaf Amidah*, on page 175. The shofar service begins with the recital of *Lam'natzayach* seven times. We are thus repeating the word Elokim (God) 49 times, purifying the 49 levels of impurity, and thereby emerging worthy of a benevolent judgment.

Min Ha-maytzar **(From out of distress)** (TR: 128). The leader recites these eight verses, one by one, and the congregation repeats them after him. The first letters of these verses combine the word *K'ra Soton*, which, loosely translated, means "abolish the adversary." It is a kabbalistic formulation reserved for this awesome service.

The Blessings. The blessing over the mitzvah of blowing the shofar is recited, followed by the blessing of *She-hecheyanu*.

The shofar is then blown following a precise order. Each blast connotes a particular emotion. It is important to refrain from idle conversation from this point until the conclusion of the services on page 263, so that we can fulfill our obligation to hear the shofar blasts in their entirety.

Page 177 (TR: 128): *Ashray Ho-om* **(Fortunate is the people).** After the initial 30 soundings of the shofar, the leader recites these three verses one by one, and we repeat after him.

King David wrote in the above Psalm: "Fortunate is the people who know the sound of the shofar." While it may be sufficient to just hear the sound of the shofar, happy is he who knows and understands its message and meaning.

 Page 177 (TR: 120): Ashrei (Happy are those), *Y'hal'lu* (Let them praise) and Returning of the Torah Scrolls to the Ark. We recite Ashray Yosh'vay (Happy are those), and the leader then says *Y'hal'lu*, and we follow with *Hodo* (His radiance). The Torah scrolls are then returned to the ark.

The Rosh Hashanah Musaf Service

 Prayerbook Pages 177 through 264

The *Musaf* service consists of the following segments:

1. The *Musaf Amidah*.

2. Additional soundings of the Shofar.

3. The leader's repetition of the *Amidah*.

4. Additional soundings of the Shofar.

5. The Priestly Blessing.

It has been noted previously that our daily prayers, as well as our Shabbat, *Rosh Chodesh*, and Festival prayers correspond to the *Korbanot* (offerings) in the *Beit Hamikdash* (Holy Temple) of old. Since on Shabbat, *Rosh Chodesh*, and the Festivals there were additional offerings (*musafim*) in the *Beit Hamikdash*, we have on these festive days a special "additional" *Amidah*, called *Musaf*.

This service begins with a silent *Amidah*, punctuated at certain points with additional blasts of the shofar, and follows with a repetition of the *Amidah* by the leader.

This prayer emphasizes three distinct concepts: *Malchiot*, *Zichronot*, and *Shofrot*. Accepting God's rulership, acknowledging that He remembers our deeds, and proclaiming that we will follow Him into the future era of *Moshiach*.

Pages 179-192: Half Kaddish, and the *Musaf Amidah*. After the Torah scrolls are returned to the ark, we remain standing for the *Musaf Amidah*. The leader then recites a special preparatory prayer, setting the tone for the service, and then recites Half Kaddish.

Before beginning the Amidah, we take three steps back, and then three steps forward, as if approaching a King.

When Rosh Hashanah occurs on Shabbat, we include the special portions marked for the Shabbat.

55

Pause at the three locations marked in the *Amidah* where the shofar is to be blown, and wait until this is done before proceeding further, except on Shabbat, since the shofar is not sounded on Shabbat.

The *Amidah* is concluded by taking three steps back, as if departing from the presence of a King, at the verse *Oseh Ha-shalom* (He who makes the peace) on page 139, and three steps forward after completing the sentence.

Pages 193-244: The Leader's Repetition of the *Musaf Amidah.* The repetition of the *Musaf Amidah* is recited by the leader. At various points during the repetition, the congregation participates by reading the portions marked Congregation. In this *Amidah*, too, the shofar is sounded at three specific locations. Note that there are different readings for the first and second days of Rosh Hashanah; this is marked in the High Holiday prayer book. As a rule, we stand whenever the ark is opened.

Page 200/223 (TR: 128): *Un'saneh Tokef* (Let us proclaim). We rise, the ark is opened, and begin reciting *Un'saneh Tokef.* This is followed by the leader who reads the last three lines aloud. We then continue *B'rosh Hashanah* (On Rosh Hashanah), and as the leader reaches the end of the paragraph, we call out in unison: *Us'shuvoh Us'filoh Utz'dokoh...* (But Repentance, Prayer and Charity...).

This poetical hymn was authored by the great martyr, Rabbi Amnon, who suffered tremendously under the hand of one Duke of Hessen some 800 years ago, when he refused to give up his Jewish faith. As he lay limbless in the synagogue on the High Holidays, he requested permission to sanctify the great name of God, and proceeded to recite this prayer. It has since become an integral part of the services.

Page 201/225 (TR: 130): *Kesser* **(A crown).** We remain standing with feet together for *Kesser.* Here the congregation recites verse by verse, followed by the leader.

Page 202/226: *L'dor* **(Through all the generations).** We may be seated once the leader begins *L'dor.*

Page 207/230 (TR: 115): *Olaynu* **(It is incumbent upon us).** All rise. The ark is opened for the prayer of *Olaynu.* As was done in the Holy Temple, when we reach the words *Va-anachnu Kor-im* (But we bend the knee), the leader and the congregation kneel and prostrate themselves for a brief moment. **To kneel:** Drop to your knees, bow forward until your forehead touches the ground, then get up.

📖 **Page 210/233** (TR: 131): *Malchiot* — The First Shofar Sounding and *Ha-yom Haras Olam* (Today is the birthday of the world). The Shofar is sounded, and we follow with the prayer of *Ha-yom Haras Olom*. The leader then resumes the repetition.

📖 **Page 213/236**: *Zichronot* — The Second Shofar Sounding and *Ha-yom Haras Olom* (Today is the birthday of the world) (TR: 131). The Shofar is sounded a second time, and we follow with the prayer of *Ha-yom Haras Olom*. The leader then resumes the repetition.

📖 **Page 215/238**: *Shofrot* — The Third Shofar Sounding and *Ha-yom Haras Olom* (Today is the birthday of the world) (TR: 131). The Shofar is sounded a third time, and we again follow with the prayer of *Ha-yom Haras Olom*. The leader then resumes the repetition.

📖 **Page 216/239** (TR: 124-125): *Modim D'rabbonon* (We thankfully acknowledge), *Ovinu Malkainu* (Our Father), and *Uch'sov* (Inscribe). Rise for *Modim*, in the middle of the page. Recite this along with the leader's recitation.

Ovinu Malkainu, Uch'sov. When the leader reaches *Ovinu Malkainu* and *Uch'sov*, we recite these verses.

The Priestly Blessing

 Prayerbook Pages 218/241

The Priestly Blessing consists of the following segments:

1. The preparation by the Kohanim.

2. The Priestly blessing.

3. Concluding prayers.

Page 218 (first day); 241 (second day): *Birchat Kohanim.* The Priestly blessing is a commandment given to the *Kohanim* (Temple priests), to bless the Jewish people with the three-fold blessing. It is the general custom that the *Kohanim* perform this duty during the *Musaf* service on Festival days, after the congregation has recited the *Modim.*

In preparation for this blessing, the *Leviim* (Levites) wash the hands of the *Kohanim* in a ritual manner. The *Kohanim* remove their shoes, and gather at the front or the eastern wall of the Synagogue.

It is customary that during the Priestly blessing men drape their prayer-shawl over their eyes, so as not to gaze upon the divine presence that rests upon the *Kohanim* when they bless the people.

59

📖 **Page 218/241** (TR: 131): *Yivorech'cho* – **The Three-fold Blessing.** After the *Kohanim* recite the benediction, the leader chants, and the *Kohanim* repeat after him, the three-fold blessing, one word at a time. When the *Kohanim* conclude each of the three verses, the congregation says *Amen.*

Ribono Shel Olom **(Master of the universe).** While the leader and the *Kohanim* are reciting the last three words of the three-fold blessing, we recite the personal request *Ribono Shel Olom.* After the *Kohanim* complete the blessing, men uncover the prayer-shawl from over their eyes. As the *Kohanim* return to their places, it is customary to thank them with the words, *Yishar Koach* (well done; thank you).

📖 **Page 220/243** (TR: 125, 132): *Uv'sayfer Cha-yim* **(And in the Book of Life) and** *Ha-yom T'amtzaynu* **(On this day).** Remain standing. When the leader recites *Uv'sayfer Cha-yim,* we recite this verse.

Ha-yom T'amtzaynu (TR: 132). The ark is opened, and we sing the hymn *Ha-yom T'amtzaynu.* Each sentence is repeated by the leader and we respond Amen and continue with the next sentence.

📖 **Pages 244-247: Whole Kaddish, Shofar Sounding and** *Ayn Kay-lokaynu* **(There is none like God).** Remain standing. The leader recites the Whole Kaddish, and the shofar is sounded again.

Ayn Kay-lokaynu (TR: 132). We recite the *Ayn Kay-lokaynu*, followed by a *Kaddish D'rabbonon* on the top of page 163.

📖 **Page 247** (TR: 115): *Olaynu* **(It is incumbent upon us) and Mourner's Kaddish** (TR: 155). We proceed with the concluding prayer, *Olaynu.*

The famous Rav Hai Gaon, the last of the Babylonian Geonim, states that the prayer of *Olaynu* was composed by Joshua, as he led the children of Israel into the Promised Land. (The initials taken from the first letter of each sentence in the first paragraph, read backwards, form his name "Hoshea.") Thus, when Joshua was about to settle the Jewish people in the Holy Land, he made them remember, through this hymn, that they were different from the Canaanite peoples and other nations and tribes of the earth, who "worship vain things and emptiness."

Mourner's Kaddish. Remain standing for the Mourner's Kaddish, recited by mourners after Olaynu.

📖 **Pages 249-263: Psalms for the day and the Final Thirty Shofar Blasts.** We conclude the service with the appropriate daily Psalms, as they are divided for the month, followed by Mourner's Kaddish. The last thirty shofar blasts, which are meant to confuse the Satan, are then sounded.

The Rosh Hashanah
Afternoon Service & Tashlich

📖 **Prayerbook Pages 267 through 292**

The afternoon service consists of the following segments:

1. Opening prayers.

2. The Torah reading [if Rosh Hashanah falls on the Shabbat].

3. The *Amidah* prayer.

4. The Leader's repetition of the *Amidah*.

5. *Ovinu Malkaynu* (Our Father, our King).

6. Concluding prayer.

7. The *Tashlich* prayer.

📖 **Page 272** (TR: 120): *Ashray* **(Happy are those).** The Psalm of Ashray can be recited while sitting.

📖 **Page 274: Half Kaddish.** Rise for the Half Kaddish, recited by the leader.

Page 275 (TR: 125-126): **Opening of the Ark and the Reading of the Torah.** On Shabbat, the ark is opened, and we recite *Va-y'hi Bin'soah* (Whenever the Ark set out). The leader recites *Gad'lu* (Exalt), and we follow with *L'cho Hashem* (Lord, yours is the greatness). The Torah is brought to the *Bima*, the reading table, and the Torah portion is read.

Lifting of the Torah (TR: 127). Once this is done, the Torah is lifted for all to see, and we recite *V'zos Ha-toroh* (This is the Torah) on page 190.

Y'hal'lu (Let them praise) and Returning of the Torah to the ark. The leader says *Y'hal'lu*, and we follow with *Hodo* (His radiance). The Torah scrolls are then returned to the ark.]

Pages 279-285: The *Amidah.* We rise for the *Amidah*, the prayer in which we put our requests to God, which begins on top of page 279 and continues through middle of page 285. Before beginning the *Amidah*, we take three steps back, and then three steps forward, as if approaching a King. It is important to note that when Rosh Hashanah occurs on Shabbat, we include the special portions marked for the Shabbat in the *Amidah*.

The *Amidah* is concluded by taking three steps back, as if departing from the presence of a King, at the verse *Oseh Ha-shalom* (He who makes the peace) on page 285, and three steps forward after completing the sentence.

📖 **Pages 279-285: The Leaders Repetition of the *Amidah*.** The repetition of the Amidah is recited by the leader.

📖 **Page 280** (TR: 132): ***Kedusha*.** Rise for *Nakdishoch* (We will hallow), near the top of the page. Here the congregation recites a paragraph, followed by the leader. Afterwards we may be seated.

📖 **Page 283** (TR: 124): ***Modim D'rabbonon* (We thankfully acknowledge).** Rise for *Modim*, in the middle of the page. Recite this along with the leader's recitation.

📖 **Page 284** (TR: 125): ***Uch'sov* (Inscribe), *Uv'sayfer Cha-yim* (And in the Book of Life) and *Ovinu Malkaynu* (Our Father, our King).** Uch'sov. When the leader reaches *Uch'sov*, we recite this verse.

Uv'sayfer Cha-yim. When the leader reaches *Uv'sayfer Cha-yim*, we recite this verse.

Ovinu Malkaynu. When Rosh Hashanah falls during the week we recite the special prayer *Ovinu Malkaynu*. This prayer is said to have been recited by Rabbi Akiva during a drought in Jerusalem, and it was the only prayer that brought rain. So, too, when we request God's mercy for our own needs, we recite this same prayer. The ark is

64

opened, and the congregation stands. This is followed by the recitation of the Whole Kaddish by the leader.

Page 289 (TR: 115): *Olaynu* (It is incumbent upon us). The concluding prayer of *Olaynu* is recited while standing.

Page 290 (TR: 155): **Mourner's Kaddish.** Remain standing for the Mourner's Kaddish recited by mourners.

Page 291 (TR: 133): **The *Tashlich* Prayer.** On the first day of Rosh Hashanah [or on the second day if the first falls on the Shabbat] it is proper to go to a body of water that contains fish – for water symbolizes kindness, and fish, an ever-open eye – and recite the Thirteen Divine Attributes of Mercy mentioned in the verses of *Mi Kayl Komocha* (Who is a God like You).

The combination of this prayer and its setting evokes in us thoughts of repentance. For it reminds us of the insecurity of fish life – the danger of fish falling for bait or getting caught in the fisherman's net. Our life, too, is full of its pitfalls and temptations. Begin by reciting the *Mi Kayl Komocha* (Who is a God like You), through the bottom of page 201. Then, men shake the four corners of their *tzitzit*. This is because the *tzitzit* reminds us of the 613 mitzvot of the Torah, and by shaking the tzitzit we are symbolically discarding all transgressions of any of these commandments.

Yom Kippur

What is Yom Kippur?

"Each year on the tenth day of the seventh month (Tishrei) you must fast and not do any work....Before God you will be cleansed of all your sins. It is a Sabbath of Sabbaths to you, and you must fast. This is a law for all time." (Lev. 16:29-31)

Yom Kippur, the holiest day of the year, is the culmination of the "Ten Days of Repentance." This is the actual day on which the eternal words, "I have forgiven," were spoken by God after Moses prayed and fasted on behalf of the Jewish people after their sin of the Golden Calf in the desert.

On Yom Kippur we receive what is perhaps God's most sublime gift: His forgiveness. When one person forgives another, it is because of a deep sense of friendship and love that overrides the effect of whatever wrong was done. Similarly, God's forgiveness is an expression of His eternal, unconditional love for every one of us.

Though we may have transgressed His will, our essence – our soul – remains Godly and pure. This is the one day when God reveals most clearly that our essence and His essence are one. Moreover, on the level of the soul, the Jewish people are all truly equal and indivisible. The more fully we demonstrate our essential unity by acting with love and friendship amongst ourselves, the more fully God's love will be revealed to us.

The Yom Kippur Services

When	What	Page in Holiday Prayer Book*
Yom Kippur Eve	Candle Lighting	18
	Kol Nidrei	23-24
	Evening Service	28-61 24-61 – When Yom Kippur begins on Friday night.
Yom Kippur Day	Morning Service	78-210
	Torah Reading	145-152
	Yizkor Service	154-155
	Musaf Service	156-210
	Priestly Blessing	203-204
Yom Kippur Afternoon	Afternoon Service	214-246
Yom Kippur Night	*Neilah* – The Concluding Service	247-273

* Kehot Hebrew/English Machzor for Yom Kippur Annotated Edition

Kol Nidrei

 ## Prayerbook Pages 35 through 36

The *Kol Nidrei* consists of the following segments:

1. Opening the Ark and taking out the Torah scrolls.

2. Reciting the Kol Nidrei.

3. Returning the Torah scrolls to the Ark.

Kol Nidrei, the prayer which ushers in the holy day of Yom Kippur, is perhaps the most famous one in our liturgy. Ironically, it is not really a prayer at all, but rather a statement. *Kol Nidrei* deals with promises, vows, and other sorts of verbal commitments commonly made in the course of the year. The Torah places strict demands on keeping one's word, and not fulfilling a vow is considered a serious misdeed. *Kol Nidrei*, which means "all vows," nullifies the binding nature of such promises in advance. One declares all future vows and promises invalid, and, as if to make absolutely sure, the vows are, "absolved, remitted, cancelled, declared null and void, not in force or in effect."

On Yom Kippur, when the soul is fully revealed, we express our real attitude towards the imperfections which might slip into our behavior – in this case, our speech – in the coming year. They are denied and declared insignificant.

69

In *Kol Nidrei*, we say it the way it is: Every Jew is in essence holy, anything unholy is null and insignificant.

📖 **Page 35** (TR: 134): *Kol Nidrei,* **Opening of the Ark.** Rise for the opening of the ark, and remain standing through the completion of *Kol Nidrei,* on bottom of page 36.

When the Torah scrolls are brought to the leader, we begin reciting *Hashem Moloch* (When the Lord will reveal) followed by *Or Zoruah* (Light is sown).

Al Da-as. Al Da-as (With the sanction) is recited three times. This verse teaches us that we are to include the transgressors of Israel in our midst – so that they may be counted among us – since all of Israel is one.

Kol Nidrei. The leader chants the *Kol Nidrei* three times, beginning with a soft voice, slowly rising with each repetition. The reason for this is that he is like one who is petitioning a king, first in a humble tone and slowly rising with confidence. We chant the *Kol Nidrei* softly, along with the leader.

📖 **Page 36:** *V'nislach* **(And may),** *S'lach* **(Pardon) and** *She-hecheyanu* **(Blessed are You).** When the leader completes the *Kol Nidrei*, he recites the verse *V'nislach* three times, and we repeat it after him. The leader then says *S'lach*, and we say the last verse, *Va-yomer*, three times.

70

She-hecheyanu. Next, men recite the blessing of *She-hecheyanu* [women have already recited it when lighting the candles], and the Torah scrolls are returned to the ark.

◆◦∋◦✷◦∈◦◆

Prayer for Welcoming the Shabbat

Prayerbook Pages 37 through 41

When Yom Kippur falls on the Shabbat, the services begin with special prayers for welcoming the Shabbat, known as *Kabbalat Shabbat.* These prayers start on the top of page 37 and continue through page 41, and are usually recited while standing.

Pages 37-39 (TR: 111): *Mizmor L'dovid* (A Psalm by David) and *Lecho Dodi* (Come my Beloved). This Psalm, recited while standing, inaugurates the Shabbat. The seven repetitions of the words *kol hashem* ("voice of the Lord") in this Psalm correspond to the seven days of Creation, when everything was created by God's word.

L'cho Dodi. This beautiful hymn, welcoming the Shabbat Queen, is recited while standing. After each paragraph we repeat the verse *L'cho Dodi.*

71

The refrain of this hymn *L'cho Dodi* and, indeed, the entire motif of the hymn, in which the Shabbat is represented as a "Queen" whom we go out to welcome, is based on a Talmudic source, where we are told how two great Sages welcomed the Shabbat. Rabbi Chanina used to dress himself in honor of Shabbat and say (to his disciples): "Come, let us go out to welcome the Shabbat Queen." Rabbi Yannai, dressed in his Shabbat clothes, would announce: "*Bo-i Chalo, Bo-i Chalo*" – Come in, Bride; come in, Bride.

Page 40 (TR: 155): **Mourner's Kaddish.** At specifically marked intervals during the prayers, when praying with a quorum of at least ten Jewish male adults, mourners recite this Kaddish. All rise for this Kaddish.

Kaddish means "holy." It was composed, like most of our prayers, by the Anshay K'nesset Hagedolah – the Men of the Great Assembly. It is based on the wording of Ezekiel's prophecy in which Kiddush Hashem, the sanctification of God's Name, is placed in the center of the national duty of Israel, upon which the deliverance of the Jewish nation was dependent.

The word *Amen*, that the congregation responds, is like the word *Emunah*, which means belief, and by stating it we acknowledge that we believe what the reader has stated.

The Yom Kippur Evening Service

Prayerbook Pages 42 through 86

The evening service consists of the following segments:

1. Half Kaddish and *Bor'chu* (Bless).

2. The *Shema* (Hear O Israel).

3. The *Amidah*.

4. Supplications

5. Concluding prayers.

When Yom Kippur falls on Shabbat, the services begin at the top of page 37 (see page 71 above).

Page 42 (TR: 113): **Half Kaddish and *Bor'chu* (Bless).** The leader recites Half Kaddish followed by *Bor'chu*. The prayer of Bor'chu is a summons, or call, by the leader to join him in praising God. It is explained in the *Zohar* or *Kabbalah*, that all mitzvot require proper preparation; we do not want to perform the sacred mitzvot like robots, without proper mental preparation. We want to pause to think of the great significance of the mitzvah we are about to perform.

This same benediction is said once again at the end of the Shabbat evening prayer, for those who may have tarried in coming to the synagogue and have not heard its first recital.

Bor'chu is recited standing, and with a special bow of the head in reverence to the One and Only God. After *Bor'chu* we may be seated.

Pages 44-45 (TR: 113): **The *Shema* (Hear, O Israel).** The *Shema*, the essence of our faith, is recited at this point. It is customary to cover our eyes with our right hand while reciting the first verse of the *Shema*, to promote deep concentration.

The verse following *Shema Yisro-ayl* (Hear O Israel), *Boruch Shaym* (Blessed be His name), normally said in an undertone, is recited here aloud, demonstrating our high spiritual standing and connection with God on the day of Yom Kippur.

The *Shema* consists of three chapters taken from the Bible. The first chapter begins with the proclamation: "Hear, O Israel, the Lord is our God, the Lord is One." It goes on to tell us that we must love God and dedicate our lives to the carrying out of His will. We can keep this faith alive only if we bring up our children in this belief. This section also contains the two mitzvot of *tefillin* and *mezuzah*, which remind us that we are Jews.

The second chapter contains a promise that if we carry out God's commands we shall be a happy people in our land. If not, we will suffer exile and hardships in strange lands, so that by suffering and trouble we will learn the ways of God and return to Him.

We are again reminded to teach our children our true faith, and the *tefillin* and *mezuzah* are again mentioned, being the symbols of practical observance of God's commands.

The third chapter contains the commandment of *tzitzit*, the distinctive Jewish garment which is a constant reminder of all the precepts of the Torah. We are reminded, also, that God brought us out of Egypt and made us His people, and that we accepted Him as our God.

Pages 47-57: The *Amidah*. We rise for the *Amidah*, the prayer in which we put forth our requests to God, and the leader first recites Half Kaddish.

Before beginning the Amidah, we take three steps back, and then three steps forward, as if approaching a King.

When Yom Kippur occurs on Shabbat, we include the special portions marked for the Shabbat in the Amidah.

Since this is the day of atonement, we add the verbal confession in the *Amidah*, from pages 37 to 41. They are arranged in the order of the Hebrew alphabet. Notice that the confessions are in the plural form. This is because the Jewish people are intrinsically united with one another, and depend on each other's spiritual well-being. We therefore not only beg for forgiveness for ourselves, but for the Jewish people as a whole.

Starting with *Oshamnu* (We have transgressed), and later, at each line of *Al Chayt* (For the sin), we tap the left side of our chest over our heart, with our right fist, for the lusts and desires of the heart lead us to sin. We should feel deep remorse for transgressing God's will, and resolve never to return to these errant ways.

The *Amidah* is concluded by taking three steps back, as if departing from the presence of a King, at the verse *Oseh Ha-shalom* (He who makes the peace) on page 41, and three steps forward after completing the sentence.

Pages 57-58 (TR: 113-114): **Shabbat Prayers.** When Yom Kippur occurs on Shabbat, we continue with *Va-y'chulu* (The heavens), near the bottom of page 57, and *Mogayn Ovos* (He was a shield), at the top of page 58; we stand for these prayers. Otherwise, we continue with *Ya-aleh* (May our supplications), near the bottom of page 58.

Va-y'chulu. By reciting *Va-y'chulu*, a Jew gives testimony that God created the heavens and the earth, and all that is in them, in six days, and rested on the seventh day, which He proclaimed a holy day of rest. The Jewish people are the living witnesses that attest to this truth, and every Jew should realize the great and unique privilege to be such a witness. Hence the *Zohar* concludes: "A Jew should give this testimony with joy and gladness of heart."

Mogayn Ovos. The words "He was a shield," "He resurrects the dead" and "the holy King" clearly refer to the familiar first three blessings of the *Amidah*. The words "for to them He decided to give rest" refer to the central Shabbat blessing *r'tzay vim'nuchoasaynu*, "please find favor in our rest."

The words "We will serve Him," "God worthy of praise" and "Master of Peace" refer to the familiar last three blessings of every *Amidah*.

Page 58 (TR: 136): *Ya-aleh* **(May our supplications).** We rise as the ark is opened, and the prayer of *Ya-aleh* is recited.

Pages 59-82: Supplications. The ark is closed and we recite prayers evoking awe and repentance. The ark is then reopened for certain prayers.

Page 61 (TR: 136): *Dark'cho* **(It is Your way) and** *Hashem, Hashem* **(Lord, Lord).** It is customary in some communities to sing the verses of *Dark'cho* and *L'ma-an'cho* (Our God). This is followed shortly by the recital of the Thirteen Divine Attributes of Mercy, *Hashem, Hashem*, which are said while standing.

The Thirteen Attributes of Mercy were revealed to Moses when he prayed for God's forgiveness for the sin of the Golden Calf. Our Sages say that on that occasion God, as it were, wrapped Himself in a *tallit*, like a leader stepping before the Ark, and said to Moses, "Thus shall you pray, saying, '*Hashem, Hashem....*'"

Thus, God showed to Moses how Jews can obtain God's forgiveness through *teshuvah* (repentance and return to God) and reciting the Thirteen Attributes of God's Mercy.

Page 65-66 (TR: 126, 136): *Hashem, Hashem* (Lord, Lord) and *Ki Hinay* (Indeed, as clay). The Thirteen Divine Attributes of Mercy, *Hashem, Hashem*, are recited again.

Ki Hinay. The ark is opened and we recite or sing the heart-warming hymn of *Ki Hinay*. It reminds us of our dependence upon God, and beseeches him to forgive us for our transgressions.

Page 67 (TR: 126): *Hashem, Hashem* (Lord, Lord). The ark is closed and the Thirteen Divine Attributes of Mercy, *Hashem, Hashem*, are recited again.

Page 70 (TR: 137): *Sh'ma Kolaynu* (Hear our voice). All rise, the ark is opened, and the leader begins the plea *Sh'ma Kolaynu*, verse by verse, and we repeat each verse after him.

Pages 71-76 (TR: 138): Verbal Confession and *V'al Kulom* (For all these). Starting with *Oshamnu* (We have transgressed), and later, at each line of *Al Chayt* (For the sin), we tap the left side of our chest over our heart, with our right fist.

V'al Kulom. Three times during the verbal confession we pause at the verse *V'al Kulom*, and recite it in unison.

Page 80 (TR: 125): *Ovinu Malkaynu* (Our Father, our King). When Yom Kippur falls during the week, we recite the special prayer *Ovinu Malkaynu*. The ark is opened, and the congregation stands.

This prayer is said to have been recited by Rabbi Akiva during a drought in Jerusalem, and it was the only prayer that brought rain. So, too, when we request God's mercy for our own needs, we recite this same prayer. The ark is opened, and the congregation stands.

Page 82 (TR: 114): *L'dovid Mizmor* (By David, a Psalm). The leader recites this Psalm, and we repeat it after him, line by line.

This Psalm is dedicated to the kingship of God. With the creation of man, God became King, for one cannot be a king if he has no subjects to rule. Adam became God's first subject and he immediately proclaimed the sovereignty of the Creator: "King of the Universe." For this reason this Psalm has been made an important part of the High Holiday prayers.

79

📖 **Pages 83-86** (TR: 115): **Whole Kaddish and *Olaynu* (It is incumbent upon us).** We remain standing, and the leader recites Whole Kaddish. We then proceed with the concluding prayer, *Olaynu*. The famous Rav Hai Gaon, the last of the Babylonian Geonim, states that the prayer of *Olaynu* was composed by Joshua, as he led the children of Israel into the Promised Land. (The initials taken from the first letter of each sentence in the first paragraph, read backwards, form his name "Hoshea.") Thus, when Joshua was about to settle the Jewish people in the Holy Land, he made them remember, through this hymn, that they were different from the Canaanite peoples and other nations and tribes of the earth, who "worship vain things and emptiness."

[When Yom Kippur falls on Shabbat, before *Olaynu* we recite *Mizmor L'dovid* (A Psalm by David), Half Kaddish and *Bor'chu* (Bless).]

📖 **Page 86** (TR: 155): **Mourner's Kaddish.** Remain standing for the Mourner's Kaddish.

The Yom Kippur Morning Service

📖 **Prayerbook Pages 115 through 298**

The morning service consists of the following segments:

1. The morning prayers.

2. The *Shema*.

3. The *Amidah*.

4. The reading of the Torah.

5. The Yizkor service.

6. The *Musaf* service.

7. The priestly blessing.

📖 **Page 115** (TR: 155): **Mourner's Kaddish and *Hodu* (Offer praise).** The Mourner's Kaddish is recited standing (page 114). We then begin *Hodu*, on top of page 115, which can be recited while sitting.

The opening prayers are mostly devoted to the expression of thanks for God's help and grace. The first part of *Hodu* comes from the first book of Chronicles. King David composed this prayer, and the famous singer Asaph and his choir sang it in the Sanctuary on the day when the Holy Ark was returned to Jerusalem.

The second section, which begins with *Shiru La-shem* (Sing to the Lord) and ends with *V'hallel La-shem* (and praise to the Lord), was said in the Temple every evening, right after the completion of the offerings. It pictures the future as promised to us in the holy Scriptures, when God will be recognized by all of mankind, and Israel will be respected as the true servants of God.

Pages 117-122: *Hashem Melech* (The Lord is King) and Psalms. At this point the congregation rises to recite *Hashem Melech*, which near the bottom of page 117. When this is completed, we may sit and continue the Psalms with *Lam'na-tzayach* (For the choirmaster). The central theme of these passages is God's reign upon all the earth. Thus, while we recognize our good fortune in that God has been especially gracious to us in bringing us close to Him, we hope and pray for the day when all the nations of the world will also acknowledge God and fear Him.

Pages 123-125 (TR: 116-118): *Hallelukah* (Praise the Lord), *Hodu La-hashem Ki Tov* (Praise the Lord) and *Hoaderes* (Power). We rise for the Psalm *Hallelukah*, at the top of page 123. Our Sages explain that the 26 verses of praise to God in *Hodu La-shem Ki Tov* allude to the 26 generations of the human race that preceded the giving of the Torah at Mt. Sinai. Since the world was created for the sake of the Torah, and without Torah it could not have existed on its own merits, the world was sustained during this period entirely by God's boundless kindness. The 26 generations (2448 years) comprise the ten generations from Adam to Noah; another ten from Noah to Abraham; and the next six generations, namely, Isaac, Jacob, Levi, Kehot, Amram and Moses.

Page 125 (TR: 119): *Boruch She-omar* (Blessed is He who spoke). Men gather the front two fringes of their prayer-shawl or *tzitzit*, and hold them in their right hand. Then the next two paragraphs in middle or page 125, *L'shaym* (For the sake) and *Boruch She-omar*, are recited. Afterwards, the fringes are kissed and released. We may be seated.

Pages 127-131 (TR: 120): *Ashray* (Happy are those) and Songs of Praise. The Psalm of *Ashray*, in the middle of page 127, introduces a series of songs of praise written by King David. We take a closer look at the beautiful world we live in, and offer praise to its maker.

Pages 131-137: *Boruch* (Blessed). Rise for *Boruch*, a set of prayers recounting our exodus from Egypt and praising God for His deliverance. Remain standing until after *Bor'chu* (Bless), at the top of page 137.

Page 136 (TR: 121, 113, 122): *Uv'Chayn Yishtabach* (And therefore), *Shir Ha-ma-alos* (A Song of Ascents), Half Kaddish, *Bor'chu* (Bless), and *Kel Adon* (Almighty God). The leader recites *Shir Ha-ma-alos*, followed by Half Kaddish and *Bor'chu*, a call to prayer. After Bor'chu we may be seated. When Yom Kippur occurs on the Shabbat, we continue with the prayers under the heading, "On Shabbat". Otherwise, continue with the section, "On weekdays."

Pages 141-143 (TR: 113): **The *Shema* (Hear, O Israel).** In preparation for the *Shema*, while reciting the words *Va-havi-aynu L'sholom* (Bring us in peace), near the top of page 141, men gather all four fringes of their prayer-shawl or tzitzit. The tzitzit are held until *Lo-ad Ka-yemet* (Abide forever), in the middle of page 142.

The *Shema*, the essence of our faith, is then recited. It is customary to cover our eyes with our right hand while reciting the first verse of the *Shema*, to promote deep concentration.

While reciting the portion of the *tzitzit*, each time we say the word *tzitzit*, we bring the tzitzit to our lips, and give them a kiss. This shows our deep reverence and love for this commandment.

Pages 145-155: The *Amidah*. We rise for the *Amidah*, the prayer in which we put forth our requests to God, which begins on the top of page 145 and continues through page 155. Before beginning the *Amidah*, we take three steps back, and then three steps forward, as if approaching a King.

When Yom Kippur occurs on Shabbat, we include the special portions marked for the Shabbat in the *Amidah*.

Since this is the day of atonement, we add the verbal confession in the *Amidah*, from pages 150 to 155. They are arranged in the order of the Hebrew alphabet. Notice that the confessions are in the plural form. This is because the Jewish people are intrinsically united with one another, and depend on each other's spiritual well-being. We therefore not only beg for forgiveness for ourselves, but for the Jewish people as a whole.

Starting with *Oshamnu* (We have transgressed), and later, at each line of *Al Chayt* (For the sin), we tap the left side of our chest over our heart, with our right fist, for the lusts and desires of the heart lead us to sin. We should feel deep remorse for transgressing God's will, and resolve never to return to these errant ways.

The *Amidah* is concluded by taking three steps back, as if departing from the presence of a King, at the verse *Oseh Ha-shalom* (He who makes the peace), on the bottom of page 155, and three steps forward after completing the sentence.

Pages 156-190: The Leader's Repetition of the Amidah. The repetition of the *Amidah* is recited by the leader. At various points during the repetition, the congregation participates by reading the portions marked Congregation. As a rule, we stand whenever the ark is opened.

📖 **Page 170** (TR: 123, 124): *L'kayl Oraych Din* **(To the Almighty who arranges judgment) and *Kedusha.*** The prayer of *L'kayl Oraych Din* is recited here. This prayer continues in the spirit of praising God. In it we cite numerous examples of God's infinite lovingkindness. Note how this prayer is written in alphabetical order (the second letter of each verse proceeding in the order of the Hebrew alphabet).

Kedusha. Rise for *Nakdishoch* (We will hallow), at the top of the page. Here, the congregation recites one verse at a time, followed by the leader.

There is a great deal of preparation going on among the angelic hosts before they utter their prayers to sanctify their Creator: *Kadosh, kadosh, kadosh* (Holy, holy, holy). *Kadosh* also means "separate"; to say that "God is holy" is to say that God is separated from, and unaffected by, the world He created.

The repetition of the word "holy" three times is explained in the Aramaic translation of the *Kedusha* in the prayer of *Uva L'tzion*: "Holy in the heavens above, the abode of His glory; holy on earth, the work of His might; holy forever and ever."

While reciting this prayer, we stand with our feet together and refrain from any interruption. Afterwards we may be seated.

Page 175: **Supplications.** We recite supplications, special prayers evoking awe and repentance.

Page 177: *Sh'ma Kolaynu* (**Hear our voice**). All rise, the ark is opened, and the leader begins the plea *Sh'ma Kolaynu*, verse by verse, and we repeat each verse after him.

Page 179 (TR: 138): **Verbal Confession and *V'al Kulom* (For all these).** Starting with *Oshamnu* (We have transgressed), and at each line of *Al Chayt* (For the sin), we tap the left side of our chest over our heart with our right fist.

V'al Kulom. Three times during the verbal confession we pause at the verse *V'al Kulom*, and recite it in unison.

Page 188 (TR: 124-125): *Modim D'rabbonon* (**We thankfully acknowledge**) and *Uch'sov* (**Inscribe**). Rise for *Modim*, in the middle of the page. Recite this along with the leader's recitation.

Uch'sov. When the leader reaches Uch'sov, we recite this verse.

Page 190 (TR: 125): *Uv'sayfer Cha-yim* (**And in the Book of Life**) and *Ovinu Malkaynu* (**Our Father, our King**). When the leader reaches *Uv'sayfer Cha-yim*, we recite this verse with him.

When Yom Kippur falls during the week we recite the special prayer *Ovinu Malkaynu*. This prayer is said to have been recited by Rabbi Akiva during a drought in Jerusalem, and it was the only prayer that brought rain. So, too, when we request God's mercy for our own needs, we recite this same prayer. The ark is opened, and the congregation stands. This is followed by the recitation of the Whole Kaddish by the leader.

Page 193 (TR: 155): **The Song of the Day and Mourner's Kaddish.** Locate and recite the Psalm that corresponds to this day of the week. It is then followed by the Mourner's Kaddish.

In the days of old, when the *Beit Hamikdash* (Holy Temple) was in existence, the *Leviim* (Levites) had an important part in the holy service conducted there daily. Their task was to sing hymns of praise to God, which they also accompanied on musical instruments. One of the highlights of the service of the Levites was the singing of the "Song of the Day." It consisted of a special Psalm from the Book of *Tehillim*, a different one for each of the seven days of the week. This has been made part of our morning service.

The Yom Kippur Torah Reading

📖 Prayerbook Pages 198-209

The Torah reading consists of the following segments:

1. Opening the ark and bringing the Torah scrolls to the *bima* or reading table.

2. Reading from the first Torah.

3. Reading from the second Torah.

4. The Haftorah.

📖 **Page 198** (TR: 125-126): **Opening of the Ark and *Va-y'hi Bin'soah* (Whenever the Ark set out).** The ark is opened, and the Torah scrolls are taken to the reading table, from which the reader will read the portion for this day.

At this point we recite *Va-y'hi Bin'soah*, *Hashem, Hashem* (Lord, Lord), and a personal request of God, *Ribono Shel Olom* (Master of the world).

Va-y'hi Bin'soah: We bless God for having given us the Torah "with His holiness." The Torah and holiness are bound together. A holy way of life is one in which everything we do is dedicated to God.

89

It is not a life of ease, but a life of service. God requires His people to be a "holy nation."

The Torah stresses: "You shall be holy; for I, your God, am holy." Thus, in the few words that comprise this short prayer, we bring up the past — Moses and the Ark; and the future — the day when all the earth will be filled with the knowledge of God. And the two are linked to the present — our dedication to the Torah in our present-day life.

Hashem, Hashem: We say this verse three times. The Thirteen Attributes of Mercy were revealed to Moses when he prayed for God's forgiveness for the sin of the Golden Calf. Our Sages say that on that occasion God, as it were, wrapped Himself in a *tallit*, like a leader stepping before the Ark, and said to Moses, "Thus shall you pray, saying, '*Hashem, Hashem....*'"

Thus, God showed to Moses how Jews can obtain God's forgiveness through *teshuvah* (repentance and return to God) and reciting the Thirteen Attributes of God's Mercy. For this reason, the Thirteen Attributes are recited during the High Holidays.

Page 199 (TR: 126): **The *Shema* (Hear).** While the Torah scrolls are held, the leader recites the verse of *Shema* (Hear), and *Echod* (Our God is One). We repeat each verse after him. The leader recites *Gad'lu* (Exalt), and we follow with *L'cho Hashem* (Lord, yours is the greatness), as the Torah scrolls are carried to the reading table.

When the Torah is taken from the Ark, it is a most appropriate time to declare our faith in the One God, for the Torah is also one and only, holy and eternal. The fact that the leader, who is our representative, makes this declaration while holding the Torah, and that we repeat it after him, is like declaring it on oath.

Pages 202-203: The Torah Reading. The Torah portions for Yom Kippur are found here. The reading in the Torah is about the solemn service in the *Beit Hamikdash* (Holy Temple) on the Day of Atonement, conducted by the High Priest himself. This was the only day in the year when the High Priest was permitted to enter the Holy of Holies to offer incense and recite a prayer there in behalf of the entire people.

Page 206 (TR: 127): Lifting of the First Torah and Reading from the Second Torah. With the conclusion of the reading from the first Torah, the Torah is lifted for all to see, and we recite *V'zos Ha-toroh* (This is the Torah). This is the same Torah which Moses placed before the children of Israel. Nothing in it has changed. It is as relevant today as it was then. The second Torah is set on the reading table, and the portion of the Torah in which God commands us regarding the observances of Yom Kippur is read.

Lifting of the Second Torah. As the Torah is lifted, we once again proclaim, *V'zos Ha-toroh* (This is the Torah).

91

Page 207: The Haftorah. The Haftorah, a selection from the Prophets, is read. The Haftorah speaks about the true meaning of repentance. The prophet urges us to approach repentance wholeheartedly, with a genuine resolve to return to the ways of the Torah. But fasting alone is not enough. "Rather, this is the fast that I will choose – loosen the fetters of wickedness...offer your bread to the hungry...." Though God is exalted and dwells on High, the prophet says, He also relates with the contrite and humble of spirit.

Furthermore, no repentance can be complete without a better appreciation and observance of the holy Shabbat: "If you restrain your feet because of the Shabbat from attending to your affairs on My holy day, and you call the Shabbat "delight"...and you honor it by not following your customary ways, refraining from pursuing your affairs and from speaking profane things, then you shall delight in the Lord...."

Page 209: *Y'kum Purkon* (May there come forth). When Yom Kippur falls on the Shabbat, after the Haftorah is completed and before Yizkor, we recite *Y'kum Purkon*, at the bottom of page 209.

The Yizkor Service

 ## Prayerbook Pages 210 through 211

Yizkor is recited by those who have lost either one or both of their parents. Others leave the synagogue until the completion of the Yizkor service; the reason for this is to advocate long life for their living parents.

The Yizkor service is much more than a service of remembrance. During Yizkor the souls of the departed descend from heaven and are joined with those who are close to them. The message they bear is clear. We are not to just remember their mortal life, but all that they stood for. The focus is primarily on the *neshamah*, the soul.

From their perspective, we are fortunate. We are alive and can still effect change in the course of our lives. We still have the ability to choose right over wrong. The departed do not.

They beseech us to follow the traditions they passed down to us — for our sake, as much as for theirs. For when we heed their call and turn toward God, we give wings to their souls, enabling them to rise to even higher spiritual heights, and we mortals gather the necessary strength to recommit ourselves to the ways of the Torah. When we take their message to heart, we have accomplished the purpose of Yizkor.

To emerge from the Yizkor service charged with a renewed commitment to living Jewishly, is to emerge successful.

📖 **Page 210** (TR: 138): *Yizkor* **(May God remember).** This paragraph is recited while standing. The first paragraph applies to fathers and the second to mothers. Be sure to recite the appropriate one – or both if necessary.

At the marked location in the prayer say your parent's Hebrew name and that of his or her mother. Then conclude by reciting Ov *Horachamim* (May the All-Merciful), which immediately follows.

📖 **Page 213:** *Y'hal'lu* **(Let them praise) and Returning of the Torah Scrolls to the Ark.** The leader says *Y'hal'lu*, and we follow with *Hodo* (His radiance). The Torah scrolls are then returned to the ark.

The Yom Kippur Musaf Service

📖 **Prayerbook Pages 212 through 298**

The *Musaf* service consists of the following segments:

1. The *Musaf Amidah*.

2. The leader's repetition of the *Amidah*.

3. The *Avodah* – A recounting of the Yom Kippur service in the Holy Temple.

4. The priestly blessing.

It has been noted previously that our daily prayers, as well as our Shabbat, *Rosh Chodesh*, and Festival prayers correspond to the *Korbanot* (offerings) in the *Beit Hamikdash* (Holy Temple) of old. Since on Shabbat, *Rosh Chodesh*, and the Festivals there were additional offerings (musafim) in the *Beit Hamikdash*, we have on these festive days a special "additional" *Amidah*, called *Musaf*.

This service begins with a silent *Amidah*, and follows with a repetition of the *Amidah* by the leader.

📖 **Pages 214-226: Half Kaddish, and the *Musaf Amidah*.** After the Torah scrolls are returned to the ark, we remain standing for the *Musaf Amidah*. The leader then recites a special preparatory prayer, setting the tone for the service, and then recites Half Kaddish. Before beginning the *Amidah*, we take three steps back, and then three steps forward, as if approaching a King.

When Yom Kippur occurs on Shabbat, we include the special portions marked for the Shabbat in the *Amidah*.

Starting with *Oshamnu* (We have transgressed), in the middle of page 221, and at each line of *Al Chayt* (For the sin), we tap the left side of our chest over our heart with our right fist.

The *Amidah* is concluded by taking three steps back, as if departing from the presence of a King, at the verse *Oseh Ha-shalom* (He who makes the peace) on bottom of page 226, and three steps forward after completing the sentence.

Pages 227-287: The Leader's Repetition of the *Musaf Amidah*. The repetition of the *Musaf Amidah* is recited by the leader. At various points during the repetition, the congregation participates by reading the portions marked Congregation. As a rule, we stand whenever the ark is opened.

Page 238 (TR: 128): *Un'saneh Tokef* (Let us proclaim). We rise, the ark is opened, and we begin reciting *Un'saneh Tokef*. This is followed by the leader who reads the last three lines aloud. We then continue *B'rosh Hashanah* (On Rosh Hashanah), and as the leader reaches the end of the paragraph, we call out in unison: *Us'shuvah Us'filah Utz'dokoh...* (But Repentance, Prayer and Charity...).

This poetical hymn was authored by the great martyr, Rabbi Amnon, who suffered tremendously under the hand of one Duke of Hessen some 800 years ago, when he refused to give up his Jewish faith. As he lay limbless in the synagogue on the High Holidays, he requested permission to sanctify the great name of God, and proceeded to recite this prayer. It has since become an integral part of the services.

Page 239 (TR: 130): *Kesser* (A crown). We remain standing for *Kesser*. Here the congregation recites verse by verse, followed by the leader.

Page 241 (TR: 131): *Ho-ochayz B'yad* (He holds in His hand). The ark is opened, and we begin reciting the hymn *Ho-ochayz B'yad*. Once this is completed, and the ark is closed, we may be seated.

Page 245 (TR: 115): *Olaynu* (It is incumbent upon us). All rise. The ark is opened for the prayer of *Olaynu*. As done in the Holy Temple, when we reach the words *Va-anachnu Kor-im* (But we bend the knee), the leader and the congregation kneel and prostrate themselves for a brief moment. **To kneel:** Drop to your knees, bow forward until your forehead touches the ground, then get up. This is done three more times during the *Avodah* recitation (below).

Pages 246-258: The *Avodah* (service). Here we recount the Yom Kippur *Avodah* as it was performed in the *Beit Hamikdash* (Holy Temple) of old. In that time, the entire Jewish people watched the *Kohein Gadol* (High Priest) perform this service, from early dawn on Yom Kippur until the end of the day, for the atonement of the entire people depended upon it.

Our sages tell us, happy were those who actually witnessed all of this. Here, at least, we can catch a glimpse of the proceedings.

Page 257 (TR: 140): ***K'ohel Hanimtach* (Like the resplendent canopy).** The poem of *K'ohel Hanimtach,* is usually sung. Following this, the focus of the prayers turns to our long and bitter exile. We no longer have the mighty Temple, and can no longer perform the services. We sorrowfully state: Because of our iniquities, we have been banished from our land. We then beseech God to rebuild for us the Temple, and return the Jewish people to the Land of Israel.

Page 272 (TR: 137): ***Sh'ma Kolaynu* (Hear our voice).** All rise, the ark is opened and the leader begins the plea *Sh'ma Kolaynu,* verse by verse, and we repeat each verse after him.

Pages 273-278 (TR: 138): **Verbal Confession and *V'al Kulom* (For all these).** Starting with *Oshamnu* (We have transgressed), and at each line of *Al Chayt* (For the sin), we tap the left side of our chest over our heart, with our right fist.

V'al Kulom. Three times during the verbal confession we pause at the verse *V'al Kulom*, and recite it in unison with the congregation.

Page 282 (TR: 124-125): ***Modim D'rabbonon* (We thankfully acknowledge).** Rise for *Modim*, in the middle of the page. Recite this along with the leader's recitation.

Page 283: *Ovinu Malkainu* (Our Father) and *Uch'sov* (Inscribe). When the leader reaches *Ovinu Malkaynu* and *Uch'sov*, we recite them.

The Priestly Blessing

Prayerbook Pages 284 through 285

The Priestly Blessing consists of the following segments:

1. The preparation by the *Kohanim*.

2. The Priestly blessing.

3. Concluding prayers.

99

Page 284 (TR: 131): ***Birchat Kohanim.*** The Priestly blessing is a commandment given to the *Kohanim* (Temple priests), to bless the Jewish people with the three-fold blessing. It is the general custom that the *Kohanim* perform this duty during the *Musaf* service on Festival days, after the congregation has recited the *Modim.*

In preparation for this blessing, the *Leviim* (Levites) wash the hands of the *Kohanim* in a ritual manner. The *Kohanim* remove their shoes, and gather at the front or the eastern wall of the Synagogue.

It is customary that during the Priestly blessing men drape their prayer-shawl over their eyes, so as not to gaze upon the divine presence that rests upon the *Kohanim* when they bless the people.

Y'vorech'cho – **The Three-fold Blessing.** After the *Kohanim* recite the benediction, the leader chants, and the *Kohanim* repeat after him, the three-fold blessing, one word at a time. When the leader concludes each of the three verses, the congregation says, Amen.

Ribono Shel Olom **(Master of the universe).** While the leader and the *Kohanim* are reciting the last three words of the three-fold blessing, we recite the personal request *Ribono Shel Olom.* After the *Kohanim* complete the blessing, men uncover the prayer-shawl from over their eyes.

As the *Kohanim* return to their places, it is customary to thank them with the words, *Yishar Koach* (well done; thank you).

Page 286 (TR: 125): *Uv'sayfer Cha-yim* (**And in the Book of Life**). Remain standing. When the leader recites *Uv'sayfer Cha-yim*, we recite this verse.

Ha-yom T'amtzaynu (**On this day**) **and Whole Kaddish.** The ark is opened, and we sing the hymn *Ha-yom T'amtzaynu.* The leader then recites the Whole Kaddish.

Pages 288-297 (TR: 155): **Psalms for the day and Mourner's Kaddish.** We conclude the service with the appropriate daily Psalms, as they are divided for the month, followed by a Mourner's Kaddish.

The Yom Kippur Afternoon Service

Prayerbook Pages 299 through 346

The afternoon service consists of the following segments:

1. The Torah reading.

2. The *Amidah* prayer.

3. The leader's repetition of the *Amidah.*

4. *Ovinu Malkaynu* (Our Father, our King).

Page 302 (TR: 125-126): **Opening of the Ark and the Reading of the Torah.** The ark is opened, and we recite *Va-y'hi Bin'soah* (Whenever the Ark set out). The leader recites *Gad'lu* (Exalt), and we follow with *L'cho Hashem* (Lord, yours is the greatness). The Torah is brought to the *Bima*, the reading table, and the Torah portion is read, pages 304-305.

The reading in the Torah speaks of the purity of Jewish life. The Torah warns us not to follow in the immoral ways of the Egyptians and native Canaanites, "that the land spew you not out also, when you defile it, as it spewed out the nations that were before you."

Page 305 (TR: 127): **Lifting of the Torah and the *Haftorah*.** Once the Torah reading is completed, the Torah is lifted for all to see, and we recite *V'zos Ha-toroh* (This is the Torah) in the middle of the page.

Haftorah. The *Haftorah* consists of the entire Book of Jonah. It contains a timely message on the importance of repentance and prayer. If sinfulness can cause the land to spew out its inhabitants, repentance can also cause the fish to deposit Jonah back on dry land and return him to life. Never should anyone despair. Prayer and repentance lead from darkness to light, from the shadow of death to a new life.

Pages 309-319: Returning of the Torah to the Ark, Half Kaddish and the *Amidah*. Once the Haftorah is completed, the leader says *Y'hal'lu*, and we follow with *Hodo* (His radiance). The Torah is then returned to the ark. This is followed by a Half Kaddish.

The *Amidah*. Before beginning the *Amidah*, we take three steps back, and then three steps forward, as if approaching a King.

[It is important to note that when Yom Kippur occurs on Shabbat, we include the special portions marked for the Shabbat in the *Amidah*.]

Since this is the day of atonement, we recite the verbal confession in the *Amidah*, from pages 315 to 319. They are arranged in the order of the Hebrew alphabet. Notice that the confessions are in the plural form. This is because the Jewish people are intrinsically united with one another, and depend on each other's spiritual well-being. We therefore not only beg for forgiveness for ourselves, but for all the Jewish people. Starting with *Oshamnu* (We have transgressed), and at each line of *Al Chayt* (For the sin), we tap the left side of our chest over our heart with our right fist, for the lusts and desires of the heart lead us to sin. We should feel deep remorse for transgressing God's will, and resolve never to return to these errant ways.

The *Amidah* is concluded by taking three steps back, as if departing from the presence of a King, at the verse *Oseh Ha-shalom* (He who makes the peace) near the bottom of page 319, and three steps forward after completing the sentence.

103

Pages 320-342: The Leader's Repetition of the *Amidah*. The repetition of the *Amidah* is recited by the leader. At various points during the repetition, the congregation participates by reading the portions marked Congregation. As a rule, we stand whenever the ark is opened.

Page 323 (TR: 132): ***Kedusha*.** Rise for *Nakdishoch* (We will hallow), in the middle of the page. Here, the congregation recites one verse at a time, followed by the leader.

There is a great deal of preparation going on among the angelic hosts before they utter their prayers to sanctify their Creator: *Kadosh, kadosh, kadosh* (Holy, holy, holy). *Kadosh* also means "separate"; to say that "God is holy" is to say that God is separated from, and unaffected by, the world He created. The repetition of the word "holy" three times is explained in the Aramaic translation of the *Kedusha* in the prayer of *Uva L'tzion*: "Holy in the heavens above, the abode of His glory; holy on earth, the work of His might; holy forever and ever."

While reciting this prayer, we stand with our feet together and refrain from any interruption. Afterwards we may be seated.

Page 326: Supplications. We recite supplications beginning with *Z'chor Rachamecho* (Lord, remember your mercies), to evoke awe and repentance.

Page 330: Sh'ma Kolaynu (Hear our voice). All rise, the ark is opened, and the leader begins the plea *Sh'ma Kolaynu*, verse by verse, and we repeat each verse after him.

Pages 331-336 (TR: 138): **Verbal Confession and *V'al Kulom* (For all these).** Starting with *Oshamnu* (We have transgressed), and at each line of *Al Chayt* (For the sin), we tap the left side of our chest over our heart with our right fist.

V'al Kulom. Three times during the verbal confession we pause at the verse V'al Kulom, and recite it in unison with the congregation.

Page 340 (TR: 124, 125): *Modim D'rabbonon* (We thankfully acknowledge) and *Uch'sov* (Inscribe). Rise for *Modim*, in the middle of the page. Recite this along with the leader's recitation.

Uch'sov. When the leader reaches *Uch'sov*, we recite this verse.

Page 342 (TR: 125): *Uv'sayfer Cha-yim* (And in the Book of Life) and *Ovinu Malkaynu* (Our Father, our King). When the leader reaches *Uv'sayfer Cha-yim*, we recite this verse with him.

When Yom Kippur falls during the week we recite the special prayer Ovinu Malkaynu. This prayer is said to have been recited by Rabbi Akiva during a drought in Jerusalem, and it was the only prayer that brought rain. So, too, when we request God's mercy for our own needs, we recite this same prayer. The ark is opened, and the congregation stands. This is followed by the recitation of the Whole Kaddish by the leader.

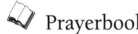 **Page 346** (TR: 155): **Mourner's Kaddish.** The service concludes with Mourner's Kaddish.

Neilah – The Concluding Service

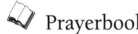 Prayerbook Pages 347 through 389

Neilah, the concluding service, consists of the following segments:

1. Opening prayers.

2. The *Amidah* prayer.

3. The leader's repetition of the *Amidah*.

4. *Ovinu Malkaynu* (Our Father, our King).

5. Declaration of our faith and the sounding of the shofar.

6. Closing prayers.

Neilah means "closing the gate." As the awesome day of Yom Kippur comes to a close, and our judgment for the coming year is being sealed, we turn to God with this final prayer while the "gates of mercy" are still open.

It is important to concentrate all our efforts on these final prayers, imploring God to accept our sincere repentance and new resolutions, and that He "seal" us in the Book of Life, granting us a new year replete with goodness and true happiness.

Page 347 (TR: 120): **Opening of the Ark and *Ashray* (Happy are those).** All rise, and the ark is opened, for the entire service. The opening prayers begin with *Ashray*.

Page 349: Half Kaddish and the *Amidah*. After the leader recites Half Kaddish, Before beginning the *Amidah*, we take three steps back, and then three steps forward, as if approaching a King.

[It is important to note that when Yom Kippur occurs on Shabbat, we include the special portions marked for the Shabbat in the *Amidah*.] Since this is the day of atonement, we recite the verbal confession in the *Amidah*, on page 355.

Starting with *Oshamnu* (We have transgressed), we tap the left side of our chest over our heart, with our right fist, for the lusts and desires of the heart lead us to sin. We should feel deep remorse for transgressing God's will, and resolve never to return to these errant ways.

107

The *Amidah* is concluded by taking three steps back, as if departing from the presence of a King, at the verse *Oseh Ha-shalom* (He who makes the peace) on page 357, and three steps forward after completing the sentence.

Pages 358-376: **The Leader's Repetition of the Amidah.** The repetition of the *Amidah* is recited by the leader. At various points during the repetition, the congregation participates by reading the portions marked Congregation.

Page 360 (TR: 141, 130): *Sha-aray Armon* (Hasten to open the gates) and *Kesser* (A Crown). We recite *Sha-aray Armon* and remain standing for *Kesser*. Here, the congregation recites one verse at a time, followed by the leader. When this is completed the leader continues reading through the top of page 259.

Page 364 (TR: 141, 126): *P'sach Lonu* (Open for us) and *Hashem, Hashem* (Lord, Lord). The leader reads one verse at a time of P'sach Lonu, and we repeat after him.

Hashem, Hashem. We then recite the Thirteen Divine Attributes of Mercy, and continue with supplications. The Thirteen Divine Attributes of Mercy are repeated three more times at marked points during the next few pages.

Page 372: *Atoh Nosayn* (You extend). The leader continues from pages 372 through page 374.

Page 374 (TR: 124, 141): *Modim D'rabbonon* (We thankfully acknowledge), *Ovinu Malkaynu* (Our Father, our King) and *Va-chasom* (Seal). Recite *Modim*, in the middle of the page, along with the leader's recitation.

Ovinu Malkaynu. We recite a special short *Ovinu Malkaynu.*

Va-chasom. Next we recite *Va-chasom.*

Page 376 (TR: 142): *Uv'sayfer Cha-yim* (And in the Book of Life) and *Ovinu Malkaynu* (Our Father, our King). When the leader reaches *Uv'sayfer Cha-yim*, we recite this verse with him. We recite the regular *Ovinu Malkaynu*. This prayer is said to have been recited by Rabbi Akiva during a drought in Jerusalem, and it was the only prayer that brought rain. So, too, when we request God's mercy for our own needs, we recite this same prayer.

Page 379 (TR: 142): **The Three Verses of Faith, Whole Kaddish and *Ayn Kaylokaynu* (There is none like God).** The apex of the service, the emotional peak, is where we announce in unison the verses proclaiming God as our God. It is written that when we recite the first of the three verses, the *shema*, every Jew should have the

109

intention of giving up their soul for the sanctification of God's name. This intention will be considered as if we had indeed withstood the test to sanctify the Divine Name.

Shema (**Hear**). The leader recites this verse and we repeat it.

Boruch Shaym (**Blessed be the name**). The leader recites this verse three times, and then we repeat it after him three times. These repetitions express that God was, is, and always will be sovereign.

Hashem Hu Ho-elokim (**God is the Lord**). The leader recites this verse seven times, and we then repeat it after him seven times. This repetition corresponds to the ascension of the added Divine Presence which has dwelt in our midst from the commencement of Yom Kippur, through the Seven Heavens.

Whole Kaddish. The leader recites this with a joyful voice, since we are certain that God has granted our pardon.

Sounding of the Shofar. Before the leader completes the Kaddish the shofar is sounded with one long blast, followed by the entire congregation rejoining with: *Leshono Habo-oh Birusholo-yim* (Next year in Jerusalem!).

Ayn Kaylokaynu **and Kaddish** (TR: 132). We then say the concluding prayers of *Ayn Kaylokaynu* followed by Kaddish *D'rabbonon*.

Page 382 (TR: 115, 155): *Olaynu* (**It is incumbent upon us**) **and Mourner's Kaddish.** The service concludes with *Olaynu* and Mourner's Kaddish.

Transliterated Prayers

Mizmor L'Dövid

Mizmor l'dövid, hövu la-donöy b'nay aylim, hövu la-donöy kövod vö-oz. Hövu la-donöy k'vod sh'mo, hish-tachavu la-donöy b'had'ras kodesh. Kol adonöy al hamö-yim, ayl ha-kövod hir-im, adonöy al ma-yim rabim. Kol adonöy bako-ach, kol adonöy be-hödör. Kol adonöy shovayr arözim, va-y'shabayr adonöy es ar'zay hal'vönon.Va-yarkidaym k'mo aygel, l'vönon v'siryon k'mo ven r'aymim. Kol adonöy cho-tzayv lahavos aysh. Kol adonöy yöchil midbör, yöchil adonöy midbar ködaysh. Kol adonöy y'cholayl a-yölos va-yechesof y'öros, uv'haychölo, kulo omayr kövod. Adonöy lamabul yöshöv,va-yayshev adonöy melech l'olöm. Adonöy oz l'amo yitayn, adonöy y'vöraych es amo va-shölom.

L'Chöh Dodi

L'chöh dodi lik'ras kalöh, p'nay shabös n'kab'löh. L'chöh dodi lik'ras kalöh, p'nay shabös n'kab'löh.

Shömor v'zöchor b'dibur echöd, hishmi-önu ayl ha-m'yuchöd, adonöy echöd ush'mo echöd, l'shaym ul'sif-eres v'lis'hilöh. L'chöh dodi lik'ras kalöh, p'nay shabös n'kab'löh.

Lik'ras shabös l'chu v'nayl'chöh, ki hi m'kor ha-b'röchöh, may-rosh mikedem n'suchöh, sof ma-aseh b'macha-shövöh t'chilöh. L'chöh dodi lik'ras kalöh, p'nay shabös n'kab'löh.

Hisna-ari may-öför kumi, liv'shi big'day sif-artaych ami, al yad ben yishai bays ha-lachmi, kör'vöh el nafshi g'ölöh. L'chöh dodi lik'ras kalöh, p'nay shabös n'kab'löh.

Hisor'ri hisor'ri, ki vö oraych kumi ori, uri uri shir da-bayri, k'vod adonöy öla-yich niglöh. L'chöh dodi lik'ras kalöh, p'nay shabös n'kab'löh.

Lo say-voshi v'lo si-köl'mi, mah tish-tochachi umah te-he-mi, böch ye-chesu ani-yay ami, v'niv-n'söh hö-ir al tilöh. L'chöh dodi lik'ras kalöh, p'nay shabös n'kab'löh.

V'höyu lim'shisöh sho-sö-yich, v'röchaku köl m'val'ö-yich, yösis öla-yich elohö-yich, kim'sos chösön al kalöh. L'chöh dodi lik'ras kalöh, p'nay shabös n'kab'löh.

Yömin us'mol tifro-tzi, v'es adonöy ta-ari-tzi, al yad ish ben par-tzi, v'nis-m'chöh v'nögilöh. L'chöh dodi lik'ras kalöh, p'nay shabös n'kab'löh.

Turn around, facing west, and say: Bo-i v'shölom ateres ba-löh, gam b'rinöh uv'tzöhölöh, toch emunay am s'gulöh, **(Bow right)** bo-i chalöh, **(Bow left)** bo-i chalöh, **(Turn back, then say silently a third time:)** bo-i chalöh shabös mal-k'sö. L'chöh dodi lik'ras kalöh, p'nay shabös n'kab'löh.

112

Response to Borchu

Böruch adonöy ha-m'voröch l'olöm vö-ed.

The Shema

It is customary to cover our eyes with our right hand while reciting the first verse of the *Shema*, in order to promote deep concentration.

Sh'ma yisrö-ayl adonöy elohaynu adonöy echöd.

Remove your hand from your eyes, and say the following in an undertone (except on Yom Kippur):

Böruch shaym k'vod mal'chuso l'olöm vö-ed.

Va-Y'chulu

Va-y'chulu ha-shöma-yim v'hö-öretz v'chöl tz'vö-öm. Va-y'chal elohim ba-yom ha-sh'vi-i, m'lachto asher ösöh, va-yishbos ba-yom ha-sh'vi-i miköl m'lachto asher ösöh. Va-y'vörech elohim es yom ha-sh'vi-i, va-y'kadaysh oso, ki vo shövas miköl m'lachto, asher börö elohim la-asos.

Mögayn Övos

Mögayn övos bid'võro m'cha-yeh maysim b'ma-amöro ha-melech ha-ködosh she-ayn kömohu ha-mayni-ach l'amo b'yom shabbas köd-sho, ki võm rötzöh l'höni-ach löhem, l'fönöv na-avod b'yir-öh vö-fachad v'no-deh lish'mo b'chöl yom tömid, may-ayn ha-b'röchos, ayl ha-hodö-os adon ha-shölom, m'kadaysh ha-shabös um'võraych sh'vi-i, umayni-ach bik'dushöh, l'am m'dush'nay oneg, zaycher l'ma-asay v'rayshis.

L'Dövid Mizmor

L'dövid mizmor, la-donöy hö-öretz um'lo-öh, tayvayl v'yosh'vay vöh. Ki hu al yamim y'södöh, v'al n'höros y'cho-n'nehöh. Mi ya-aleh v'har adonöy, umi yökum bim'kom kö-dsho. N'ki cha-pa-yim uvar layvöv, asher lo nösöh lashöv nafshi, v'lo nish'ba l'mirmöh. Yisöh v'röchöh may-ays adonöy utz'dököh may-elohay yish-o. Zeh dor dor'shöv, m'vak'shay fönechö ya-akov selöh. S'u sh'örim röshaychem v'hi-nös'u pis'chay olöm v'yövo melech ha-kövod. Mi zeh melech ha-kövod adonöy izuz v'gibor, adonöy gibor milchömöh. S'u sh'örim röshaychem us'u pis'chay olöm v'yövo melech ha-kövod. Mi hu zeh melech ha-kövod, adonöy tz'vö-os hu melech ha-kövod selöh.

Ölaynu

Ölaynu l'shabay-ach la-adon ha-kol, lösays g'dulöh l'yo-tzayr b'rayshis, shelo ösönu k'go-yay hö-arötzos, v'lo sömönu k'mish-p'chos hö-adömöh, shelo söm chelkaynu köhem, v'gorölaynu k'chöl ha-monöm she-haym mishtachavim l'hevel v'lörik. Va-anachnu kor'im umishtachavim umodim, lif'nay melech, mal'chay ha-m'löchim, ha-ködosh böruch hu. She-hu no-teh shöma-yim v'yosayd öretz, umoshav y'köro ba-shöma-yim mima-al, ush'chinas uzo b'göv'hay m'romim, hu elohaynu ayn od. Emes malkaynu, efes zulöso, kakösuv b'soröso: V'yöda-tö ha-yom vaha-shayvosö el l'vövechö, ki adonöy hu hö-elohim ba-shöma-yim mima-al, v'al hö-öretz mi-töchas, ayn od.

V'al kayn n'kaveh l'chö adonöy elohaynu lir-os m'hayröh b'sif-eres uzechö, l'ha-avir gilulim min hö-öretz v'hö-elilim köros yiköray-sun, l'sakayn olöm b'mal'chus shadai, v'chöl b'nay vösör yik-r'u vish'mechö, l'hafnos ay-lechö köl rish'ay öretz. Yakiru v'yayd'u köl yosh'vay sayvayl, ki l'chö tichra köl berech, tishöva köl löshon. L'fönechö adonöy elohaynu yich-r'u v'yipolu, v'lich'vod shim'chö y'kör yitaynu, vi-kab'lu chulöm alayhem es ol mal'chusechö, v'simloch alayhem m'hayröh l'olöm vö-ed, ki ha-mal'chus shel'chö hi, ul'ol'may ad timloch b'chövod, ka-kösuv b'sorösechö, adonöy yimloch l'olöm vö-ed. V'ne-emar, v'hö-yöh adonöy l'melech al köl hö-öretz, ba-yom ha-hu yih-yeh adonöy echöd ush'mo echöd.

115

Greeting for Rosh Hashanah

To a Man: L'shönö tovöh tikö-sayv v'say-chösaym.

To a Woman: L'shönö tovöh tikö-sayvi v'say-chösaymi.

Hodu La-Donöy Ki Tov

Hodu la-donöy ki tov, ki l'olöm chasdo.

Hodu lay-lohay hö-elohim, ki l'olöm chasdo.

Hodu la-adonay höadonim, ki l'olöm chasdo.

L'osay niflö-os g'dolos l'vado, ki l'olöm chasdo.

L'osay ha-shöma-yim bi-s'vunöh, ki l'olöm chasdo.

L'roka hö-öretz al ha-mö-yim, ki l'olöm chasdo.

L'osay orim g'dolim, ki l'olöm chasdo.

Es ha-shemesh l'mem-sheles ba-yom, ki l'olöm chasdo.

Es ha-yöray-ach v'cho-chövim l'mem-sh'los ba-löy-löh, ki l'olöm chasdo.

L'makay mitzra-yim biv'choray-hem, ki l'olöm chasdo.

Va-yo-tzay yisrö-ayl mitochöm, ki l'olöm chasdo.

B'yöd chazököh uviz'ro-ah n'tuyöh, ki l'olöm chasdo.

L'gozayr yam suf lig'zörim, ki l'olöm chasdo.

V'he-evir yisrö-ayl b'socho, ki l'olöm chasdo.

V'ni-ayr par-oh v'chaylo v'yam suf, ki l'olöm chasdo.

L'molich amo bamidbör, ki l'olöm chasdo.

L'makay m'löchim g'dolim, ki l'olöm chasdo.

Va-yaharog m'löchim adirim, ki l'olöm chasdo.

L'sichon melech hö-emori, ki l'olöm chasdo.

Ul'og melech ha-böshön, ki l'olöm chasdo.

V'nösan ar-tzöm l'na-chalöh, ki l'olöm chasdo.

Na-chalöh l'yisrö-ayl avdo, ki l'olöm chasdo.

Sheb'shiflaynu zöchar lönu, ki l'olöm chasdo.

Va-yif-r'kaynu mitzöraynu, ki l'olöm chasdo.

Nosayn lechem l'chöl bösör, ki l'olöm chasdo.

Hodu l'ayl ha-shömö-yim, ki l'olöm chasdo.

Hö-Aderes V'Hö-Emunöh

Hö-aderes v'hö-emunöh, l'chai olömim.

Ha-binöh v'ha-b'röchöh, l'chai olömim.

Ha-ga-avöh v'hag'dulöh, l'chai olömim.

Ha-day-öh v'hadibur, l'chai olömim.

Ha-hod v'he-hödör, l'chai olömim.

Ha-va-ad v'ha-vösikus, l'chai olömim.

Ha-ziv v'ha-zohar, l'chai olömim.

Ha-chayil v'ha-chosen, l'chai olömim.

Ha-teches v'ha-tohar, l'chai olömim.

Ha-yichud v'ha-yir-öh, l'chai olömim.

Ha-keser v'ha-kövod, l'chai olömim.

Ha-lekach v'ha-libuv, l'chai olömim.

Ha-m'luchöh v'ha-memshölöh, l'chai olömim.

Ha-noy v'ha-nay-tzach, l'chai olömim.

Ha-siguy v'hasegev, l'chai olömim.

Hö-oz v'hö-anövöh, l'chai olömim.

Ha-p'dus v'ha-p'ayr, l'chai olömim.

Ha-tz'vi v'ha-tzedek, l'chai olömim.

Ha-k'ri-öh v'ha-k'dushöh, l'chai olömim.

Hö-ron v'höro-maymos, l'chai olömim.

Ha-shir v'ha-shevach, l'chai olömim.

Ha-t'hilöh v'ha-tif-eres, l'chai olömim.

Böruch She-Omar

Böruch she-ömar v'hö-yöh hö-olöm, böruch hu, böruch omayr v'o-seh, böruch gozayr um'ka-yaym, böruch o-seh v'rayshis, böruch m'ra-chaym al hö-öretz, böruch m'ra-chaym al ha-b'ri-yos, böruch m'shalaym söchör tov liray-öv, böruch chai lö-ad v'kayöm lö-netzach, böruch po-deh umatzil, böruch sh'mo. Böruch atöh adonöy elohaynu melech hö-olöm, hö-ayl, öv höra-chamön, ha-m'hulöl b'feh amo, m'shuböch um'fo-ör bil'shon chasidöv va-avödoöv, uv'shi-ray dövid av-dechö. N'ha-lel'chö adonöy elohaynu, bish'vöchos uviz'miros. N'gadel'chö un'shabay-chachö un'fö-er'chö, v'namlich'chö v'nazkir shim'chö malkaynu elohaynu, yöchid, chay hö-olömim, melech. M'shuböch um'fo-ör, aday ad sh'mo ha-godol. Böruch atöh adonöy, melech m'hulöl batish-böchos.

Men kiss the strings of the Tallit (fringed garment/prayer shawl).

Ashray Yosh'vay

Ash-ray yosh'vay vay-sechö, od y'hal'luchö selöh. Ash-ray hö-öm sheköchö lo, ash-ray hö-öm she-adonöy elohöv. T'hilöh l'dövid aromi-m'chö elohai ha-melech, va-avö-r'chöh shim'chö l'olöm vö-ed. B'chöl yom avö-r'chekö, va-aha-l'löh shim'chö l'olöm vö-ed. Gödol adonöy um'hulöl m'od, v'lig'dulöso ayn chayker. Dor l'dor y'shabach ma-asechö, ug'vurosechö yagidu. Hadar k'vod ho-dechö, v'div'ray nif-l'osechö ö-sichöh. Ve-ezuz nor'osechö yomayru, ug'dulös'chö asap'renöh. Zecher rav tuv'chö yabi-u, v'tzid'kös'chö y'ra-naynu. Chanun v'rachum adonöy, erech apa-yim ug'döl chösed. Tov adonöy lakol, v'ra-chamöv al köl ma-asöv. Yoduchö adonöy köl ma-asechö, va-chasi-dechö y'vör'chuchö. K'vod mal'chus'chö yomayru, ug'vurö-s'chö y'da-bayru. L'hodi-ah liv'nay hö-ödöm g'vurosöv, uch'vod hadar mal'chuso. Mal'chus'chö, mal'chus köl olömim, umemshalt'chö b'chöl dor vödor. Somaych adonöy l'chöl ha-nof'lim, v'zokayf l'chöl ha-k'fufim. Aynay chol aylechö y'sa-bayru, v'atöh nosayn löhem es öchlöm b'ito. Posay-ach es yödechö, umas-bi-a l'chöl chai rö-tzon. Tzadik adonöy b'chöl d'röchöv, v'chösid b'chöl ma-asöv. Körov adonöy l'chöl kor'öv, l'chol asher yikrö-uhu ve-emes. R'tzon y'ray-öv ya-aseh, v'es shav-ösöm yish-ma v'yoshi-aym. Shomayr adonöy es köl ohavöv, v'ays köl hör'shö-im yashmid. T'hilas adonöy y'daber pi, vivöraych köl bösör shaym köd-sho l'olöm vö-ed. Va-anachnu n'voraych yöh, may-atöh v'ad olöm, ha-l'luyöh.

Ha-L'luyöh

Ha-l'luyöh. Ha-l'lu ayl b'köd-sho, ha-l'luhu bir'ki-ah uzo. Ha-l'luhu big'vurosöv, ha-l'luhu k'rov gudlo. Ha-l'luhu b'sayka shoför, ha-l'luhu b'nayvel v'chinor. Ha-l'luhu b'sof umöchol, ha-l'luhu b'minim v'ugöv. Ha-l'luhu b'tzil-tz'lay shöma, ha-l'luhu b'tzil-tz'lay s'ru-öh. Kol ha-n'shömöh t'halayl yöh, ha-l'luyöh. Kol ha-n'shömöh t'ha-layl yöh, ha-l'luyöh.

Uv'Chayn Yishtabach

Uv'chayn yish-tabach shim'chö lö-ad malkaynu, hö-ayl, ha-melech, ha-gödol v'haködosh, ba-shöma-yim uvö-öretz. ki l'chö nö-eh adonöy elohay-nu vay-lohay avosaynu l'olöm vö-ed. Shir ush'vöchöh, ha-layl v'zimröh, oz umemshölöh, ne-tzach, g'dulöh ug'vuröh, t'hilöh v'sif-eres, k'dushö umal'chus. B'röchos v'hodö-os, l'shim'chö ha-gödol v'ha-ködosh umayolöm ad olöm, atöh ayl. Böruch atöh adonöy, ayl melech, gödol um'hulöl ba-tishböchos, ayl ha-hodö-os, adon ha-niflö-os boray köl ha-n'shömos, ribon köl ha-ma-asim, ha-bochayr b'shiray zimröh, melech yöchid chay hö-olömim.

Shir HaMaalos

Shir ha-ma-alos, mima-amakim k'rösichö adonöy. Adonöy shim'öh v'koli, tih-yenöh öznechö kashuvos l'kol ta-chanunöy. Im avonos tishmör yöh, adonöy mi ya-amod. Ki im'chö ha-s'lichöh, l'ma-an tivöray. Kivisi adonöy kiv'söh nafshi, v'lid'vöro hochölti. Nafshi la-donöy mi-shom'rim laboker, shom'rim laboker. Yachayl yisrö-ayl el adonöy, ki im adonöy ha-chesed v'harbay imo f'dus. V'hu yifdeh es yisrö-ayl mikol avonosöv.

Ayl Ödon

Ayl ödon al köl ha-ma-asim, böruch um'voröch b'fi köl ha-n'shömöh, gö-dlo v'tuvo mölay olöm, da-as us'vunöh sov'vim hodo.

Ha-misgö-eh al cha-yos ha-kodesh, v'neh-dör b'chövod al ha-merkövöh, z'chus umishor lif'nay chis-o, chesed v'rachamim mölay ch'vodo.

Tovim m'oros, sheböröh elohaynu, y'tzöröm b'da-as b'vinöh uv'haskayl, ko-ach ug'vuraöh nösan böhem, lih-yos mosh'lim b'kerev tay-vayl.

M'lay-im ziv um'fikim nogah, nö-eh zivom b'chöl hö-olöm, s'maychim b'tzaysöm v'sösim b'vo-öm, osim b'aymöh r'tzon konöm.

P'ayr v'chövod nos'nim lish'mo, tzö-hölöh v'rinöh l'zaycher mal'chuso, körö la-shemesh va-yizrach or, rö-öh v'hiskin tzuras ha-l'vönöh.

Shevach nos'nim lo köl tz'ö möröm, tif-eres ug'dulöh, s'röfim v'cha-yos v'ofa-nay ha-kodesh.

Nakdishöch

Nak-dishöch v'na-ari-tzöch k'no-am si-ach sod sar'fay kodesh, ha-m'shal'shim l'chö k'dushöh, ka-kösuv al yad n'vi-echö, v'körö zeh el zeh v'ömar. Wait for leader.

Ködosh, ködosh, ködosh, adonöy tz'vö-os, m'lo chöl hö-öretz k'vodo. Öz b'kol ra-ash gödol adir v'chözök, mashmi-im kol, misna-s'im l'umas ha-s'röfim, l'umö-söm m'shab'chim v'om'rim. Wait for leader.

Böruch k'vod adonöy mim'komo. Mim'komöch malkaynu sofi-ah v'simloch ölaynu ki m'chakim anach'nu löch. Mösai tim'loch b'tziyon, b'körov b'yömaynu l'olöm vö-ed. Tishkon tisgadayl v'siska-daysh b'soch y'rushöla-yim ir'chö, l'dor vödor ul'naytzach n'tzöchim. V'ay-naynu sir-enöh mal'chu-sechö, ka-dövör hö-ömur b'shiray uzechö, al y'day dövid m'shi-ach tzidkechö. Wait for leader.

Yimloch adonöy l'olöm elohayich tziyon ldor vö-dor ha-l'luyöh. Wait for leader.

Atöh V'Chartönu

Atöh v'chartönu mi-köl hö-a-mim, öhavtöh osönu v'rö-tzisö bönu, v'romam-tönu miköl ha-l'shonos, v'kidash-tönu b'mitzvo-sechö, v'kayrav-tönu malkaynu la-avodö-sechö, v'shim'chö ha-gödol v'ha-ködosh ölaynu körösö.

123

Modim

Modim anach-nu löch, shö-atöh hu adonöy elo-haynu vay-lohay avosaynu, elohay köl bösör, yo-tz'raynu, yo-tzayr b'rayshis. B'röchos v'hodö-os l'shim'chö ha-gödol v'haködosh, al she-heche-yisönu v'kiyam-tönu. Kayn t'cha-yaynu us'ka-y'maynu v'se-esof gölu-yosay-nu l'chatz'ros köd-shechö, v'nöshuv ay-lechö lishmor chukechö, v'la-asos r'tzonechö, ul'öv-d'chö b'layvöv shölaym, al she-önu modim löch. Böruch ayl ha-hodö-os.

L'Ayl Oraych Din

L'ayl oraych din. L'vochayn l'vövos b'yom din, l'go-leh amukos ba-din. L'dovayr mayshörim b'yom din, l'ho-geh day-os ba-din.. L'vösik v'o-seh chesed b'yom din, l'zochayr b'riso ba-din. L'chomayl ma-asöv b'yom din, l'tahayr chosöv ba-din. L'yoday-a macha-shövos b'yom din, l'chovaysh ka-so ba-din. L'lovaysh tz'dökos b'yom din, l'mochayl avo-nos ba-din. L'norö s'hilos b'yom din, l'solay-ach la-amusöv ba-din. L'o-neh l'kor'öv b'yom din, l'fo-ayl rachamöv ba-din. L'tzo-feh nistöros b'yom din, l'ko-neh avödöv ba-din. L'rachaym amo b'yom din, l'shomayr o-havöv ba-din. L'somaych t'mimöv b'yom din.

Uch'sov

Uch'sov l'cha-yim tovim köl b'nay v'risechö.

Uv'sayfer Cha-yim

Uv'sayfer cha-yim b'röchöh v'shölom ufarnösöh tovöh, y'shu-öh v'nechömöh, ug'zayros tovos, ni-zöchayr v'nikösayv l'fönechö, anach-nu v'chöl am'chö bays yisrö-ayl, l'cha-yim tovim ul'shölom.

Övinu Malkaynu

Övinu malkaynu, ayn lönu melech elö ötöh. Övinu malkaynu, chönaynu, va-a-naynu ki ayn bönu ma-asim. Asay imönu tz'dököh vö-chesed v'hoshi-aynu.

Va-y'hi Bin'soa Hö-öron

Va-y'hi bin'so-a hö-öron va-yomer mosheh. Kumöh adonöy, v'yöfu-tzu o-y'vechö, v'yönusu m'san'echö mi-pönechö. Ki mitzi-yon tay-tzay soröh, ud'var adonöy miru-shölö-yim. Böruch shenösan toröh l'amo yisrö-ayl bik'dushöso.

Bay Anö Röchitz

Bay anö röchitz, v'lish'may kadishö yakirö anö ay-mar tushb'chön. Y'hay ra-avö ködömöch d'siftach libö-i b'oray'sö, v'sashlim mish-alin d'libö-i, v'libö d'chöl amöch yisrö-ayl, l'tav ul'cha-yin v'lish'löm.

Adonöy, Adonöy

Adonöy, adonöy, ayl rachum v'chanun, erech apa-yim, v'rav chesed ve-emes. No-tzayr chesed lö-alöfim, nosay övon vöfesha v'chatö-öh v'na-kay.

Sh'ma

Wait for leader and respond: Sh'ma yisrö-ayl adonöy elohaynu adonöy echöd. Wait for leader and respond: Echöd elohaynu, gödol ado-naynu, ködosh v'norö sh'mo. Wait for leader and respond: L'chö adonöy ha-g'dulöh v'hag'vuröh v'ha-tif-eres v'hanay-tzach v'ha-hod, ki chol bashöma-yim uvö-öretz. L'chö adonöy ha-mamlöchöh v'ha-misnasay l'chol l'rosh. Ro-m'mu adonöy elohaynu v'hishtachavu la-hadom rag-löv ködosh hu. Ro-m'mu adonöy elohaynu v'hish-tachavu l'har köd-sho, ki ködosh adonöy elohaynu.

V'zos Ha-Toröh

V'zos ha-toröh asher söm mosheh lif'nay b'nay yisrö-ayl. Aytz cha-yim hi la-machazikim böh, v'som'chehö m'ushör. D'röchehö dar'chay no-am, v'chöl n'sivo-sehö shölom. Orech yömim bi-minöh, bis'molöh osher v'chövod. Adonöy chöfaytz l'ma-an tzidko, yagdil toröh v'ya-dir.

The Shofar Service

This psalm is recited seven times: Lam'natzay-ach liv'nay korach, mizmor. Köl hö-amim tik'u chöf, höri-u laylohim b'kol rinöh. Ki adonöy el-yon norö, melech gödol al köl hö-öretz. Yad-bayr amim tach-taynu ul'umim tachas rag-laynu. Yivchar lönu es na-chalösaynu, es g'on ya-akov asher öhayv, selöh. Ölöh elohim bis'ru-öh, adonöy b'kol shoför. Zam'ru elohim, za-mayru, zam'ru l'mal-kaynu, za-mayru. Ki melech köl hö-öretz elohim, zam'ru maskil. Mölach elohim al go-yim, elohim yöshav al kisay köd-sho. N'divay amim ne-esöfu, am elohay avröhöm, ki lay-lohim möginay eretz, m'od na-alöh.

Wait for leader to recite each verse and repeat:

Min ha-may-tzar körösi yöh, ö-nöni va-merchav yöh.

Koli shim'öh k'chas-dechö adonöy, k'mishpö-techö cha-yayni.

Rosh d'vör'chö emes, ul'olöm köl mishpat tzid-kechö.

127

Arov av-d'chö l'tov al ya-ash'kuni zaydim.

Sös önochi al im-rösechö, k'mo-tzay shölöl röv.

Tuv ta-am vöda-as lam'dayni, ki v'mitzvo-sechö he-emanti.

Nid'vos pi r'tzay nö, adonöy, umishpötechö lam'dayni.

Ölöh elohim bis'ru-öh, adonöy b'kol shoför.

After the blowing of the Shofar the leader recites the following. Wait for leader to recite each verse and repeat:

Ash-ray hö-öm yod'ay s'ru-öh, adonöy b'or pönechö y'ha-laychun.

B'shim'chö y'gilun köl ha-yom, uv'tzid'kös'chö yörumu.

Ki sif-eres uzömo ötöh, uvir'tzon'chö törum kar-naynu.

Un'saneh Tokef

Un'saneh tokef k'dushas ha-yom, ki hu norö v'ö-yom. Uvo si-nösay mal'chusechö, v'yikon b'chesed kis-echö, v'sayshayv ölöv be-emes. Emes ki atöh hu da-yön umochi-ach, v'yoday-a vö-ayd, v'chosayv v'chosaym, v'sofayr umo-neh, v'sizkor köl ha-nish-köchos. V'siftach es sayfer ha-zichronos, umay-aylöv yiköray, v'chosöm yad köl ödöm bo. Uva-shoför gödol yitöka, v'kol d'mömöh daköh yishöma. Umal-öchim yay-chöfayzun, v'chil ur'ödöh yo-chayzun, v'yom'ru hinay yom ha-din, lifkod al tz'vö mörom ba-din, ki lo yiz-ku v'aynechö ba-din. V'chöl bö-ay olöm ya-av'run l'fönechö kiv'nay

128

möron. K'vaköras ro-eh edro, ma-avir tzo-no tachas shiv-to, kayn ta-avir v'sis-por v'sim-neh, v'sifkod nefesh köl chöy, v'sachtoch kitz-vöh l'chöl bir-yosechö, v'sichtov es g'zar dinöm.

B'rosh ha-shönöh yikö-sayvun, uv'yom tzom kippur yay-chösaymun, kamöh ya-av'run, v'chamöh yiböray-un. Mi yich-yeh, umi yömus. Mi v'kitzo, umi lo v'kitzo. Mi va-ma-yim, umi vö-aysh. Mi va-cherev, umi va-cha-yöh. Mi vörö-öv, umi va-tzömö. Mi vöra-ash, umi vama-gayföh. Mi va-chaniköh, umi vas'kilöh. Mi yönu-ach, umi yönu-a. Mi yishökayt, umi yitörayf. Mi yishölayv, umi yis-yasör. Mi yay-öni, umi yay-öshayr. Mi yishö-fayl, umi yörum.

Us'shuvöh, us'filöh, utz'dököh, ma-avirin es ro-a ha-g'zayröh. Ki k'shim'chö kayn t'hilö-sechö, kösheh lich-os v'no-ach lir'tzos. Ki lo sach-potz b'mos ha-mays, ki im b'shuvo midar'ko v'chö-yöh. V'ad yom moso t'cha-keh lo, im yöshuv mi-yad t'kab'lo. Emes ki atöh hu yo-tz'röm, v'atöh yoday-a yitz-röm, ki haym bösör vödöm. Ödöm y'sodo may-öför v'sofo le-öför. B'nafsho yövi lach-mo. Möshul k'cheres ha-nishbör, kechötzir yövaysh, uch'tzitz novayl, k'tzayl ovayr, uch'önön kölöh, uch'ru-ach noshöves, uch'övök poray-ach, v'cha-chalom yö-uf. V'atöh hu melech ayl chai v'ka-yöm.

Keser

Keser yit'nu l'chö adonöy elohaynu mal-öchim ha-monay ma-löh v'am'chö yisrö-ayl k'vutzay matöh, yachad kulöm k'dushöh l'chö y'sha-layshu ka-kösuv al yad n'vi-echö v'körö zeh el zeh v'ömar. **Wait for leader.**

Ködosh, ködosh, ködosh, adonöy tz'vö-os m'lo chöl hö-öretz k'vodo. K'vodo mölay olöm m'shö-r'söv sho-alim zeh lö-zeh, a-yay m'kom k'vodo l'ha-ari-tzo, l'umösöm m'shab'chim v'om'rim. **Wait for leader.**

Böruch k'vod adonöy mim'komo. Mim'komo hu yifen b'rachamöv l'amo, ha-m'yachadim sh'mo erev vövoker b'chöl yom tömid, pa-ama-yim b'ahavöh sh'ma om'rim. **Wait for leader.**

Sh'ma yisrö-ayl, adonöy elohaynu, adonöy echöd. Hu elohaynu, hu övinu, hu malkaynu, hu moshi-aynu, hu yoshi-aynu v'yig-ölaynu shaynis b'körov, v'yashmi-aynu b'rachamöv l'aynay köl chai lay-mor, hayn gö-alti es'chem a-charis kiv'rayshis lih-yos löchem lay-lohim. **Wait for leader.**

Ani adonöy elo-haychem.**Wait for leader.** Yimloch adonöy l'olöm eloha-yich tziyon l'dor vödor, ha-l'lu-yöh.

Hö-Ochayz B'Yad

Hö-ochayz b'yad mi-das mish-pöt. V'chol ma-aminim she-hu ayl emu-nöh, ha-bochayn uvodek gin'zay nis-töros. V'chol ma-aminim she-hu bochayn k'lö-yos, ha-go-ayl mimö-ves ufo-deh mi-shachas. V'chol ma-aminim she-hu go-ayl chözök, ha-dön y'chidi l'vö-ay olöm. V'chol ma-aminim she-hu da-yön emes, he-höguy b'eh-yeh asher eh-yeh.

Ha-Yom Haras Olöm

Ha-yom haras olöm, ha-yom ya-amid ba-mishpöt köl y'tzuray olömim, im k'vönim im ka-avödim. Im k'vönim, Ra-chamaynu k'rachaym öv al bönim. V'im ka-avödim ay-naynu l'chö s'luyos, ad shet'chönaynu v'so-tzi chö-or mish-pötaynu, ö-yom ködosh.

The Priestly Blessing

Y'vörech'chö. Adonöy. V'yish-m'rechö. (**Cong.**: Ömayn.) Yö-ayr. Adonöy. Pönöv. Ay-lechö. Vi-chunekö. (**Cong.**: Ömayn.) Yisö. Adonöy. Pönöv. Ay-lechö. V'yösaym. L'chö. Shölom. (**Cong.**: Ömayn.)

Ha-Yom T'am'tzaynu

Ha-yom t'am'tzaynu. (Ömayn). Ha-yom t'vö-r'chaynu. (Ömayn).
Ha-yom t'gad'laynu. (Ömayn). Ha-yom tid-r'shaynu l'tovöh. (Ömayn).
Ha-yom tish-ma shav-ösaynu. (Ömayn). Ha-yom t'ka-bayl b'rachamim
uv'rö-tzon es t'filösaynu. (Ömayn). Ha-yom tis-m'chaynu bi-min
tzidkechö. (Ömayn).

Ayn Kaylohaynu

Ayn kaylo-haynu, ayn kado-naynu, ayn k'malkaynu, ayn
k'moshi-aynu. Mi chaylo-haynu, mi chado-naynu, mi ch'malkaynu, mi
ch'moshi-aynu. No-deh laylo-haynu, no-deh lado-naynu, no-deh
l'malkaynu, no-deh l'moshi-aynu. Böruch elo-haynu, böruch
adonaynu, böruch malkaynu, böruch moshi-aynu. Atöh hu elohaynu,
atöh hu ado-naynu, atöh hu malkaynu, atöh hu moshi-aynu, atöh
soshi-aynu. Atöh sökum t'rachaym tzi-yon ki ays l'chen'nöh ki vö
mo-ayd. Atöh hu adonöy elohaynu vay-lohay avo-saynu, she-hiktiru
avosaynu l'fönechö es k'tores ha-samim.

Nakdishöch

Nak-dishöch v'na-ari-tzöch k'no-am si-ach sod sar'fay kodesh,
ha-m'shal'shim l'chö k'dushöh, ka-kösuv al yad n'vi-echö, v'körö zeh
el zeh v'ömar. **Wait for leader.**

Ködosh, ködosh, ködosh, adonöy tz'vö-os, m'lo chöl hö-öretz k'vodo. **Wait for leader.**

Böruch k'vod adonöy mim'komo. **Wait for leader.**

Yimloch adonöy l'olöm, eloha-yich tziyon, l'dor vö-dor, ha-l'luyöh. **Wait for leader**.

The Tashlich Prayer

Mi ayl kömo-chö, nosay övon v'ovayr al pesha lish'ayris na-chalöso lo hechezik lö-ad apo, ki chöfaytz chesed hu. Yöshuv y'ra-chamay-nu yich-bosh avono-saynu, v'sashlich bim'tzulos yöm köl chato-söm. Titayn emes l'ya-akov chesed l'avrö-höm asher nishba-tö la-avosaynu mi-may kedem. Min ha-may-tzar körösi yöh, ö-nöni va-merchav yöh. Adonöy li lo irö, mah ya-aseh li ödöm. Adonöy li b'oz'röy va-ani er-eh v'son'öy. Tov la-chasos ba-donöy mi-b'to-ach bö-ödöm. Tov la-chasos ba-donöy mib'to-ach bi-n'divim.

Ra-n'nu tza-dikim ba-donöy, la-y'shörim nö-vöh s'hilöh. Hodu la-donöy b'chinor, b'nayvel ösor zam'ru lo. Shiru lo shir chödösh, haytivu na-gayn bis'ru-öh. Ki yöshör d'var adonöy, v'chöl ma-asayhu be-emunöh. Ohayv tz'dököh umish-pöt, chesed adonöy mö-l'öh hö-öretz. Bid'var adonöy shöma-yim na-asu, uv'ru-ach piv köl tz'vö-öm. Konays kanayd may ha-yöm, nosayn b'o-tzöros t'homos. Yi-r'u may-adonöy köl hö-öretz, mimenu yöguru köl yosh'vay sayvayl. Ki hu ömar va-yehi, hu tzivöh va-ya-amod. Adonöy hayfir atzas

133

go-yim, hay-ni mach-sh'vos amim. Atzas adonöy l'olöm ta-amod, mach-sh'vos libo l'dor vödor. Ashray ha-goy asher adonöy elohöv, hö-öm böchar l'nachalöh lo. Mishöma-yim hibit adonöy, rö-öh es köl b'nay hö-ödöm. Mim'chon shivto hishgi-ach, el köl yosh'vay hö-öretz. Ha-yo-tzayr yachad liböm, ha-mayvin el köl ma-asayhem. Ayn ha-melech noshö b'röv chö-yil, gibor lo yinö-tzayl b'röv ko-ach. Sheker ha-sus lis'shu-öh, uv'rov chay-lo lo y'malayt. Hinay ayn adonöy el y'ray-öv, la-m'yachalim l'chasdo. L'hatzil mi-mö-ves nafshöm, ul'cha-yosom börö-öv. Nafshaynu chik'söh ladonöy, ezraynu umöginay-nu hu. Ki vo yis-mach li-baynu, ki v'shaym köd-sho vötöch-nu. Y'hi chas-d'chö adonöy ölaynu ka-asher yichal-nu löch. Lo yöray-u v'lo yash-chisu b'chöl har köd-shi, ki mö-l'öh hö-öretz day-öh es adonöy kama-yim la-yöm m'chasim.

The Kol Nidrei Prayers

Adonöy mölöch tögayl hö-öretz, yis-m'chu i-yim rabim. Önön va-aröfel s'vivöv, tzedek umish-pöt m'chon kis-o. Aysh l'fönöv taylaych, us'la-hayt söviv tzöröv. Hay-iru v'rököv tayvayl, rö-asöh va-töchel hö-öretz. Hörim ka-donag nömasu mi-lif'nay adonöy, mi-lif'nay adon köl hö-öretz. Higidu ha-shöma-yim tzid-ko, v'rö-u chöl hö-amim k'vodo. Yay-voshu köl ov'day fesel ha-mis-ha-l'lim bö-elilim, hish-tachavu lo köl elohim. Shö-m'öh va-tismach tziyon, va-tögayl-nö b'nos y'hudöh, l'ma-an mish-pötechö adonöy. Ki atöh adonöy el-yon

134

al köl hö-öretz, m'od na-alaysö al köl elohim. O-havay adonöy sin'u rö, shomayr naf'shos chasidöv, mi-yad r'shö-im yatzilaym. Or zöru-a la-tzadik, ul'yish'ray layv sim-chöh. Sim'chu tzadikim ba-donöy, v'hodu l'zaycher köd-sho. Wait for leader.

Say quietly, following the leader: Köl nid-ray ve-esöray, ush'vu-ay, va-charömay, v'konömay, v'kinusay, v'chi-nu-yay. D'in-darnö, ud'ishta-ba-nö, ud'acharim-nö, ud'ösar-nö al naf-shösönö. Mi-yom kipurim zeh, ad yom kipurim ha-bö ölaynu l'tovöh. B'chul'hon i-charatnö v'hon, kul'hon y'hon shörön, sh'vikin, sh'visin, b'taylin um'vutölin, lö sh'ririn. v'lö ka-yömin. Nid-rönö lö nid-ray, ve-esörönö lö esöray, ush'vu-ösönö lö sh'vu-os. Repeat three times

Wait for leader, then say the following: V'nislach l'chöl adas b'nay yisrö-ayl v'lagayr ha-gör b'sochöm, ki l'chöl hö-öm bish'gögöh.

Leader: S'lach nö la-avon hö-öm ha-zeh k'godel chasdechö, v'cha-asher nösö-söh lö-öm ha-zeh mimitzra-yim v'ad haynöh. V'shöm ne-emar.

Cong.: (Say three times). Va-yomer adonöy sölachti kid-vörechö.

Ya-Aleh

Ya-aleh ta-chanu-naynu may-erev, v'yövo shav-ösaynu mi-boker, v'yayrö-eh rinu-naynu ad örev. Ya-aleh ko-laynu may-erev, v'yövo tzid'kösaynu mi-boker, v'yayrö-eh fid-yo-naynu ad örev. Ya-aleh inu-yaynu may-erev, v'yövo s'lichö-saynu mi-boker, v'yayrö-eh na-akösaynu ad örev. Ya-aleh m'nusaynu may-erev, v'yövo l'ma-ano mi-boker, v'yayrö-eh chipu-raynu ad örev. Ya-aleh yish-aynu may-erev, v'yövo ta-haray-nu mi-boker, v'yayrö-eh chinu-naynu ad örev. Ya-aleh zichro-naynu may-erev, v'yövo vi-udaynu mi-boker, v'yayrö-eh ha-d'rösaynu ad örev. Ya-aleh döf'kaynu may-erev, v'yövo gi-laynu mi-boker, v'yayrö-eh ba-köshö-saynu ad örev. Ya-aleh en'kösaynu may-erev, v'yövo ay-lechö mi-boker, v'yayrö-eh ay-laynu ad örev.

Dark'chö

Dar-k'chö elohaynu l'ha-arich a-pechö lörö-im v'la-tovim, v'hi s'hilösechö. L'ma-an'chö elohaynu a-say v'lo lönu, r'ay amidö-saynu dalim v'raykim.

Ki Hinay

Ki hinay ka-chomer b'yad ha-yo-tzayr, bir'tzoso mar-chiv uvir'tzoso m'katzayr, kayn anachnu b'yöd'chö chesed no-tzayr, la-b'ris ha-bayt v'al tayfen la-yaytzer. Ki hinay kö-even b'yad

136

ha-m'satays, bir'tzoso ochayz uvir'tzoso m'chatays, kayn anachnu b'yöd'chö m'cha-yeh um'mosays, la-b'ris ha-bayt v'al tayfen la-yaytzer. Ki hinay kagarzen b'yad he-chörösh, bir'tzoso di-bayk lö-or uvir'tzoso pay-rash, kayn anachnu b'yöd'chö tomaych öni vörösh, la-b'ris ha-bayt v'al tayfen la-yaytzer. Ki hinay ka-hegeh b'yad ha-malöch, bir'tzoso ochayz uvir'tzoso shi-lach, kayn anachnu b'yöd'chö ayl tov v'salöch, la-b'ris ha-bayt v'al tayfen la-yaytzer. Ki hinay ki-z'chuchis b'yad ha-m'zagayg, bir'tzoso cho-gayg uvir'tzoso m'mogayg, kayn anachnu b'yöd'chö ma-avir zödon v'shogayg, la-b'ris ha-bayt v'al tayfen la-yaytzer. Ki hinay ka-y'ri-öh b'yad ha-rokaym, bir'tzoso m'yashayr uvir'tzoso m'akaym, kayn anachnu b'yöd'chö ayl kano v'nokaym, la-b'ris ha-bayt v'al tayfen la-yaytzer. Ki hinay ka-kesef b'yad ha-tzorayf, bir'tzoso m'sagsayg uvir'tzoso m'tzörayf, kayn anachnu b'yöd'chö mam-tzi l'mözor teref, la-b'ris ha-bayt v'al tayfen la-yaytzer.

Sh'ma Kolaynu

Wait for leader and recite: Sh'ma kolaynu, adonöy elohaynu, chus v'ra-chaym ölaynu, v'kabayl b'rachamim uv'rö-tzon es t'filösaynu.

Wait for leader and recite: Ha-shi-vaynu adonöy aylechö v'nöshuvöh, chadaysh yömaynu k'kedem.

Wait for leader and recite: Al tashli-chaynu mil'fönechö, v'ru-ach köd-sh'chö al tikach mi-menu.

Wait for leader and recite: Al tashli-chaynu l'ays zik-nöh, kich'los kochaynu al ta-az'vaynu.

137

V'al Kulöm

V'al kulöm, elo-ah s'lichos, s'lach lönu, m'chöl lönu, ka-payr lönu.

The Yizkor Services

One who's father passed away says:
Yizkor elohim nish'mas abö mori (**Mention his Hebrew name and that of his mother**) she-hölach l'olömo, ba-avur sheb'li neder etayn tz'dököh ba-ado, bis'char zeh t'hay naf'sho tz'ruröh bitz'ror ha-cha-yim, im nish'mas avröhöm yitzchök v'ya-akov, söröh rivköh röchayl v'lay-öh, v'im sh'ör tzadikim v'tzidköni-yos she-b'gan ayden, v'nomar: Ömayn. **Continue below.**

One who's mother passed away says:
Yizkor elohim nish'mas imi morösi (**Mention her Hebrew name and that of her mother**) shehöl'chöh l'olömöh, ba-avur sheb'li neder etayn tz'dököh ba-adöh, bis'char zeh t'hay naf'shöh tz'ruröh bitz'ror ha-cha-yim, im nish'mas avröhöm yitzchök v'ya-akov, söröh rivköh röchayl v'lay-öh, v'im sh'ör tzadikim v'tzidköni-yös she-b'gan ayden, v'nomar: Ömayn. **Continue below.**

Continue here:
Öv höra-chamim shochayn m'romim, b'rachamöv höatzumim, hu yifkod b'rachamim, ha-chasidim v'ha-y'shörim v'hat'mi-mim, k'hilos

ha-kodesh she-mös'ru nafshöm al k'dushas ha-shaym, ha-ne-ehövim v'han'imim b'cha-yayhem, uv'mosöm lo nifrödu, min'shörim kalu, umayarö-yos gövayru, la-asos r'tzon konöm v'chayfetz tzuröm. Yizk'raym elo-haynu l'tovöh, im sh'ör tzadikay olöm, v'yinkom nik'mas dam avödöv ha-shöfuch. Ka-kösuv b'soras mosheh ish hö-elohim. Harninnu go-yim amo, ki dam avödöv yikom, v'nököm yöshiv l'tzöröv, v'chiper ad'möso amo. V'al y'day avödechö ha-n'vi-im kösuv laymor, V'nikaysi dömöm lo nikaysi, va-donöy shochayn b'tziyon. Uv'chis'vay ha-kodesh ne-emar, Lömöh yom'ru ha-go-yim a-yay elo-hayhem, yivöda ba-go-yim l'aynaynu nik'mas dam avödechö ha-shöfuch. V'omayr: Ki doraysh dömim osöm zöchör, lo shö-chach tza-akas anövim. V'omayr, Yödin ba-go-yim mölay g'vi-yos möchatz rosh al eretz raböh. Mi-nachal ba-derech yish-teh, al kayn yörim rosh.

Im'ru Laylohim

Im'ru lay-lohim. Ayl melech b'olömo, may-chish p'dus amo, l'ka-yaym d'var no-amo, ki s'lichöh imo, hodu lado-nöy kir'u vish'mo. Im'ru lay-lohim. Böruch um'hulöl b'rov göd-lo, maychish s'lichöh lik'hölo, l'har-os lakol göd-lo, mödad ma-yim b'shö-ölo, shiru lo zam'ru lo. Im'ru lay-lohim. Go-ayl am k'dosho, bis'lichöh l'hakdisho, um'cho-nayn bays mik-dösho, l'zera avrö-höm k'dosho, his-ha-l'lu b'shaym köd-sho. Im'ru lay-lohim. Dögul m'shuböch bir'ki-a uzo, solay-ach l'am zo b'zo, bid'var uzo umö-uzo, lö-chayn adas mö-uzo, dir'shu adonöy v'uzo.

139

V'Hakohanim

V'ha-kohanim v'hö-öm hö-om'dim bö-azöröh, k'she-hö-yu shom'im es ha-shaym ha-nich-böd v'ha-norö, m'forösh yo-tzay mipi cho-hayn gödol bik'dushöh uv'töhöröh, hö-yu kor'im (**bow here**) umish-tachavim v'nof'lim al p'nayhem, v'om'rim: Böruch shaym k'vod mal'chuso l'olöm vö-ed.

K'Ohel Hanimtach

K'ohel ha-nim-tach b'döray ma-löh, mar-ay cho-hayn. Kiv'rökim ha-yotz'im miziv ha-cha-yos, mar-ay cho-hayn. K'godel g'dilim b'arba k'tzövos, mar-ay cho-hayn. Kid'mus ha-keshes b'soch he-önön, mar-ay cho-hayn. K'hod asher hil-bish tzur li-tzurim, mar-ay cho-hayn. K'vered ha-nösun b'soch ginas chemed, mar-ay cho-hayn. K'zayr ha-nösun al may-tzach melech, mar-ay cho-hayn. K'chesed ha-nitan al p'nay chösön, mar-ay cho-hayn. K'tohar ha-nösun bitz'nif töhor, mar-ay cho-hayn. K'yoshayv b'sayser l'chalos p'nay melech, mar-ay cho-hayn. K'cho-chöv ha-nogah big'vul miz-röch, mar-ay cho-hayn.

Sha-aray Armon

Sha-aray armon, m'hayröh siftach l'vo-aray das ömon. Sha-aray g'nuzim, m'hayröh sif-tach l'dös'chö achu-zim. Sha-aray hay-chöl ha-neche-mödim, m'hayröh sif-tach liv'u-dim. Sha-aray z'vul machanö-yim, m'hayröh sif-tach l'chach-lilay ay-növim. Sha-aray töhöröh, m'hayröh sif-tach l'yöföh uvöröh. Sha-aray keser ha-m'yumön, m'hayröh sif-tach l'am lo al'mön. Uvöhem tu-arötz v'sukdosh, k'sod si-ach sar'fay kodesh, ha-makdishim shim'chö ba-kodesh.

P'sach Lönu Sha-ar

P'sach lönu sha-ar, b'ays n'ilas sha-ar, ki fönöh yom. Ha-yom yifneh, ha-shemesh yövo v'yifneh, növo-öh sh'örechö. Önö ayl nö, sö nö, s'lach nö, m'chal nö, chamöl nö, rachem nö, kaper nö, k'vosh chayt v'övon.

Va-Chasom

Va-chasom l'cha-yim tovim köl b'nay v'ri-sechö.

Uv'sayfer Cha-yim

Uv'sayfer cha-yim b'röchöh v'shölom ufar'nösöh tovöh, y'shu-öh v'nechömöh, ug'zayros tovos, ni-zöchayr v'naychösaym l'fönechö, anach-nu v'chöl am'chö bays yisrö-ayl, l'cha-yim tovim ul'shölom.

The Three Verses of Faith

Say one time: Sh'ma yisrö-ayl, adonöy elohaynu, adonöy echöd.

Say three times: Böruch shaym k'vod mal'chuso l'olöm vö-ed.

Say seven times: Adonöy hu hö-elohim.

L'Shönöh Habö-öh

L'shönöh habö-öh biru-shölö-yim.

Inspirational Readings & Stories

The Ultimate Car Wash

Most of us have been at a car wash at least once in our lives. The ones that are the most fun, for kids and adults alike, are the kind where you remain in the car, shift into neutral and float along on the conveyor belt.

First, there's a spray of water from one side, then the soap hits the car from somewhere else, and for an additional $1.50 you can get some hot wax so that the shine lasts longer. Finally, big rubber pieces envelop the car and dry it without so much as a scratch. Thirty seconds after this wash cycle has begun, you're driving out looking like a million bucks. That is, until you realize that the inside of your car still has windows that are smudged from the inside, cookie crumbs or candy wrappers on the floor, even a few loose coins in the seat.

The only way to get the inside clean is to open up your door and let some guy with a bottle of Windex and a vacuum cleaner jump in and do the rest of the job.

On Rosh Hashanah we all go to the synagogue, sit down, position ourselves in neutral and wait for the conveyor belt to begin moving. The rabbi zaps you from this side, the cantor and/or choir gets you from the other side, then comes the *shofar* blowing ceremony, the sermon and the Torah reading, and before you know it, the service is over.

Many of us walk out of *shul* on Rosh Hashanah feeling like a million bucks, all clean and shiny and new. But then it hits us. We aren't any cleaner on the inside than when we walked in. All of those faults and bad habits we had promised ourselves we'd change are still with us. And no amount of sitting in the synagogue, no matter how much the seats cost, is going to change us.

How can we change? Unlike our cars, unfortunately, it isn't a matter of letting someone in with rags and cleaning solution. It's much more difficult because we're the only ones who can really make sure that our insides get cleaned. Which isn't to say that change has to be a solitary experience. Certainly it is easier when we have help and support from the people around us.

Like a car wash, however, getting our insides clean is intrinsically tied up with "opening up." Once we're open to change, we're halfway there. This season of the High Holidays is the time when we contemplate our past behavior, our involvement in Judaism, our goals and values. It is a most appropriate time to begin making the necessary changes in our lives. Open up. Try something new. Attend a Torah study class. Read a Jewish book. Clean up your insides. Then you'll look and feel like a million bucks.

(Based on a Rosh Hashanah talk by Rabbi Yitzchak Sapochinsky, Chabad of Westlake Village.)

Sounding the Shofar

The sounding of the shofar contains an allusion: Awake, you sleepers, from your sleep, and you slumberers, arise from your slumber – examine your deeds, repent and remember your Creator. Those of you who forgot the truth in the vanities of the time and dwell all year in emptiness, look into your souls, improve your ways and action*s (Maimonides, Hilchot Teshuvah, Ch. 3).*

Rabbi Saadia Gaon gives ten reasons for sounding the shofar on Rosh Hashanah, among them: At the beginning of a reign, it is customary to sound trumpets before the newly crowned king, and to proclaim his ascent to sovereignty throughout the realm. Similarly, we accept anew the Creator's sovereignty upon ourselves each year on Rosh Hashanah. Also, sounding the shofar on Rosh Hashanah causes us to recall our faith in the future resurrection of the dead. As it is said: "All you inhabitants of the world, and you who dwell in the earth; when an ensign is lifted on the mountains you will see, and when the shofar is sounded you will hear." (Isaiah 18)

When the Jewish people hear the shofar, they are capable of bringing about the final Redemption. When they sound their shofars in fulfillment of the mitzvah of Rosh Hashanah, their hearts are opened, they shudder over their sins, and in a brief moment their reflections turn to repentance. They barely conclude their shofar blast and the sound of the shofar of Moshiach is already heard. The shofar sounds blend – his and theirs – and behold, Redemption comes. *(From Book of Our Heritage by Rabbi E. Kitov)*

From the Rosh Hashanah Prayers

"May everything that has been made know that You made it." (Amidah)

In the future, when Moshiach comes, every creation in this world will understand and recognize that there is a Godly power within which makes it exist and gives it its life-force. This is the meaning of this prayer which we say on Rosh Hashanah. We beseech God to reveal His Kingship in this world – "May everything that has been made know that You made it" – because in truth nothing exists without this Godliness. (Rabbi Shneur Zalman of Liadi)

"This is the day which is the beginning of Your work." (Musaf Amidah)

The world was created on the 25th of Elul. Rosh Hashanah, the first of Tishrei, is, therefore, the sixth day of Creation. How, then, can we say about Rosh Hashanah, "This is the day which is the beginning of Your work"?

The fact of the matter is that the entire purpose of Creation was to make a "dwelling place below" for God and this is accomplished through man. Because of this, before man was created, it is impossible to say that the world existed in the true sense, for its purpose was still missing. Therefore, the sixth day of Creation, on which man was created, is "the beginning of Your work" (Likutei Torah).

From the Yom Kippur Prayers

"For the sin that we have sinned." (*Amidah*)

When confessing our sins it is customary to tap the chest with our fist just over the heart, as a symbol of repentance as each transgression is enumerated. Yet logically the opposite would seem to make more sense: Should not the heart strike out at the hand that actually committed the sin? Our intention, however, is the source of all transgression – the lusts and desires of the heart that lead to sin. (Hegyonot Shel Ami)

"For with You is forgiveness, that You may be feared." (Supplications)

How does being forgiven lead us to fear God? Would not God's perpetual mercy have the opposite effect on a person, knowing that he will always be forgiven? This may be explained as follows: A poor person who has borrowed a large sum of money is only able to pay back half of the loan, not in one lump payment, but in many smaller payments stretched out over several years.

If the lender accepts these terms and is kindly and understanding, the borrower is far more likely to exert himself to try to repay the entire amount.

If, however, the lender is intransigent, insisting that the entire loan be repaid immediately, the borrower will despair of ever being able to return the full sum. The lender's kindness and mercy, therefore, lead the borrower to fear him all the more. (Lubavitcher Rebbe)

A Yizkor to Remember
by Rabbi Eugene Lebovitz

Shlomo Rosenberg and Maurice Schechter glanced at each other as they checked in at El Al's boarding gate in Heathrow International Airport, London, and then proceeded to find seats in the waiting area. Shlomo walked behind Maurice through the jetway to the plane. They had been assigned adjacent seats.

The plane departed London for Tel Aviv at 6:00 a.m., as the sun was rising over the eastern horizon. When the darkness dissipated under the face of sparkling morning rays, Shlomo took his tallit and tefillin from the overhead bin and slowly inched his way to the back of the plane where a minyan was forming for the morning service.

When he returned to his seat, he tapped Maurice on the shoulder and queried: "Would you like to borrow my tallit and tefillin before I put them away?"

Maurice glowered: "Let me tell you something! I don't need your tallit and tefillin, nor anybody else's. I have nothing to do with Him. When they," he slowed his speech and pointed to the earth below,

"When they took my youngest son, when they told me to go the right and shoved my son to the left, from that time until this day, I have no use for Him!"

"It was presumptuous of me to interfere with your private thoughts," whispered Shlomo. "But we can still talk about other matters. After all, we are both going to Israel. But let me ask you just one more question: If you are so angry with God, why are you going to Israel?"

"What do you mean, why am I going to Israel?" Maurice sputtered. "I am angry at God, but not at His people. I love the Jewish people, and I want to spend time with them, especially during this season of the year. Now, on the condition that we don't talk about Him, we can be friends."

By the time the music over the audio system reverberated with the rhythm of "Havaynu Shalom Aleichem" and the big jet touched down at Ben Gurion Airport, Shlomo and Maurice had become friends. Clearing customs, they decided to share a cab to Jerusalem. Shlomo anxiously watched pedestrians as the cab zoomed up and down the streets of Jerusalem until it stopped in front of the King David Hotel. Breathlessly, he alighted, paid half the fare, and the cab lurched forward without giving him an opportunity to ask Maurice where he was staying.

This was Shlomo's fifth annual trip to Jerusalem for Rosh Hashanah, Yom Kippur, and Sukkot. When his wife passed away six years ago, he decided to spend these holidays in the Holy City. On his first trip, he found a small shul near where he stayed. Its cantor had a sweet voice and davened with great fervor. He loved the cantor and, therefore, he returned each year.

Between Rosh Hashanah and Yom Kippur, Shlomo walked the streets of Jerusalem, always keeping his eyes open for his new friend Maurice, but they never met. During a break in the service before Yizkor on Yom Kippur, Shlomo walked toward a park. It was not far from the shul, and he thought that he would be able to rest under a shady tree.

Sitting on a bench, he recognized Maurice, who was eating a sandwich. "Listen, I know that you are angry at God, that you want to having nothing to do with Him. The fact that you are eating on Yom Kippur is your business. But, your son, what did he do that you refuse to recite a prayer in his memory?" Maurice turned sullenly away.

"You promised," he reminded Shlomo, and immediately scowled into stony silence. Shlomo sat on the bench next to Maurice, helpless to respond. Surprisingly, after a few minutes that seemed like an eternity, Maurice blurted out: "You might be right. I thought about it. It is true that I said goodbye to Him in Auschwitz, but I never said goodbye to my son. Maybe it is time to say a prayer in his memory." Maurice tearfully turned to Shlomo and whispered, "Can I go to shul with you?"

150

The two men clutched each other as they walked back. Silently each said his Yizkor and then joined the line of people waiting patiently for their turn to request the cantor to recite an individual Kayl Molay Rachamim in memory of their loved ones.

As the line grew shorter, Maurice and Shlomo inched forward. Finally, Maurice was standing face to face with the cantor. "Please, recite a Kayl Molay Rachamim for my son," Maurice said brokenly.

"What was your son's name," queried the cantor gently.

"His name was Pinchas ben Moshe," replied Maurice.

The cantor started to chant the Kayl Molay Rachamim, but stopped. "Tell me again," he insisted, "what was your son's name?"

"Pinchas ben Moshe."

"Tateh! Tateh! (Father, father)," cried the cantor, "I have been waiting for you for so long!"

Quick How-To Guides

Pesicha - Opening the Ark

1) Rise and proceed to the ark. Once there, stand facing the ark.

2) When indicated, open the curtain (and doors) and remain standing.

3) When the congregation has completed the special prayer, remove the Torah (the *Gabbai* will usually indicate which one), hold it upright with both hands, and lean it on your right shoulder.

4) Bring and give the Torah to the *Chazzan*, prayer leader, and return to your seat.

Aliyah - Going up for a Torah portion

1) Rise and proceed to the reading table where to Torah is being read.

2) Approach the Torah on the right side of the reader. The Torah will be opened and the portion that will be read will be indicated to you. Take the *Gartel* (Torah belt) and touch the scroll at the beginning and end of where it will be read, then kiss the *Gartel*.

3) Put the *Gartel* down and roll the Torah closed. Recite aloud the blessing while holding the two Torah handles, one in each hand. Allow time for the congregation to answer *Amen*, after each blessing.

4) After the blessing, the Torah will be opened. Remain standing in position while the reader reads the portion. During this time hold the right Torah handle with your right hand and try to follow along silently.

5) At the conclusion of the reading, take the *Gartel* and touch the end and beginning of the portion just read. Kiss the *Gartel*, put it down, and roll the Torah closed.

6) Recite aloud the final blessing, while holding the Torah handles with both of your hands. When you have concluded the blessing, move to the right side of the reading table and remain standing there until the next person has completed his portion and blessings. He will then take your place at the side of the reading table, and you should return to your seat.

Haggbah - Lifting the Torah

1) Rise and proceed to the reading table where to Torah is being read.

2) Stand in front of the Torah, and when indicated, roll open the Torah to a span of at least three columns. Take the *Gartel* (Torah belt) and pass it over the Torah portions, touching the Torah. Kiss the *Gartel* and put it down.

3) Hold both Torah handles, and bring the Torah forward, bringing the handles just off the table.

4) Bear down, and with one motion, lift the Torah upright, keeping it spread open. Turn right, then left, displaying the scroll to the congregation.

5) Place the Torah back on the reading table, and roll it closed. Lift it up and sit down behind you. Another person will dress the Torah with its garments.

6) Remain sitting until indicated to return the Torah to the Ark. Once there, give the Torah to the person standing there, and he will place it in the Ark. You may now return to your seat.

Gelilah - Dressing the Torah

1) Rise and proceed to the reading table where to Torah is being held.

2) Make sure the Torah is rolled closed, with a column seam at the center.

3) Take the belt and secure it around the Torah. It should rest on the lower third.

4) Put the mantel on the Torah, with the front facing away from you, followed by the other ornaments.

5) Return to your seat.

Mourner's Kaddish

Yis-gadal v'yis-kadash sh'may raböh. (Cong: Ömayn)

B'öl'mö di v'rö chir'u-say v'yamlich mal'chusay, v'yatzmach pur-könay vikörayv m'shi-chay. (Cong: Ömayn)

B'cha-yay-chon uv'yomaychon uv'cha-yay d'chöl bays yisrö-ayl, ba-agölö uviz'man köriv v'im'ru ömayn.

(Cong: Ömayn. Y'hay sh'mayh rabö m'vörach l'ölam ul'öl'may öl'ma-yö, yisböraych.)

Y'hay sh'mayh rabö m'vörach l'ölam ul'öl'may öl'ma-yö. Yisböraych, v'yishtabach, v'yispö-ayr, v'yisromöm, v'yis-nasay, v'yis-hadör, v'yis-aleh, v'yis-halöl, sh'may d'kud-shö b'rich hu. (Cong: Ömayn)

L'aylö min köl bir'chösö v'shirösö, tush-b'chösö v'ne-chemösö, da-amirön b'öl'mö, v'im'ru ömayn. (Cong: Ömayn)

Y'hay sh'lömö rabö min sh'ma-yö, v'cha-yim tovim ölaynu v'al köl yisrö-ayl v'im'ru ömayn. (Cong: Ömayn)

Take three steps back: O-seh ha-shölom bim'romöv, hu ya-aseh shölom ölaynu v'al köl yisrö-ayl, v'im'ru ömayn. Take three steps forward. (Cong: Ömayn)

Kaddish D'rabonon

Yis-gadal v'yis-kadash sh'may raböh. (Cong: Ömayn)

B'öl'mö di v'rö chir'u-say v'yamlich mal'chusay, v'yatzmach pur-könay viköray v m'shi-chay. (Cong: Ömayn)

B'cha-yay-chon uv'yomaychon uv'cha-yay d'chöl bays yisrö-ayl, ba-agölö uviz'man köriv v'im'ru ömayn.

(Cong: Ömayn. Y'hay sh'mayh rabö m'vörach l'ölam ul'öl'may öl'ma-yö, yisböraych.)

Y'hay sh'mayh rabö m'vörach l'ölam ul'öl'may öl'ma-yö. Yisböraych, v'yishtabach, v'yispö-ayr, v'yisromöm, v'yis-nasay, v'yis-hadör, v'yis-aleh, v'yis-halöl, sh'may d'kud-shö b'rich hu. (Cong: Ömayn)

L'aylö min köl bir'chösö v'shirösö, tush-b'chösö v'ne-chemösö, da-amirön b'öl'mö, v'im'ru ömayn. (Cong: Ömayn)

Al yisrö-ayl v'al rabönön, v'al tal-midayhon, v'al köl tal-miday sal-midayhon, v'al köl mön d'ös'kin b'oray'sö, di v'asrö hö-dayn, v'di v'chöl asar va-asar. Y'hay l'hon ul'chon sh'lömö rabö, chinö v'chisdö v'rachamin v'cha-yin arichin, um'zonö r'vichö ufur'könö, min ködöm avu-hon divi-sh'ma-yö v'im'ru ömayn. (Cong: Ömayn)

Y'hay sh'lömö rabö min sh'ma-yö, v'cha-yim tovim ölaynu v'al köl yisrö-ayl v'im'ru ömayn. (Cong: Ömayn)

Take three steps back: O-seh ha-shölom bim'romöv, hu ya-aseh shölom ölaynu v'al köl yisrö-ayl, v'im'ru ömayn. Take three steps forward. (Cong: Ömayn)

Index to Transliterations

Synagogue Glossary

Aliyah: Being called up to the Torah.
Amidah (lit., "standing"): Silent Prayer.
Aron Kodesh (lit., "holy ark"): Ark where the Torah is stored.
Bimah (lit., "stage"): Reading Table.
Birkat Kohanim: Preistly Blessing.
Chazzan (lit., "cantor"): Prayer Leader.
Ezrat Noshim: Women Section.
Gabbai: Organizer; assistant.
Gellilah: Binding the Torah.
Haftorah: Portion from the Prophets.
Hagboh: Lifting the Torah.
Kaadish: Special Mourner's Prayer.
Kippah: Head covering.
Kittle: Special garment worn on Yom Kippur.
Maariv: Evening Service.
Machzor: Holiday Prayer book.
Mechitza: Partition.
Mincha: Afternoon Service.
Minyan: Quorum of ten adult Jewish males.
Parasha: Portion.
Poroches: Curtain covering the ark.
Shacharit: Morning Service.
Shtender: Prayer stand.
Siddur: Prayer Book.
Taalit: Prayer shawl.
Tehillim: Psalms, the book of.
Yarmulka: Head covering.

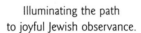

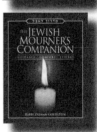